BUSINESS
WRITING
MADE EASY

BUSINESS
WRITING
MADE EASY

SUZAN ST MAUR

bookshaker

First Published in Great Britain 2011
by www.BookShaker.com

© Copyright Suzan St Maur

To my "HowToWriteBetter" *subscribers*

Thank you for appreciating my help!

FOREWORD

"You can rob me... you can starve me, you can beat me, and you can kill me... just don't bore me."

**Clint Eastwood, as Sgt. Gunny Highway,
in *Heartbreak Ridge* (1986)**

ONE OF MY PET PEEVES is business writing that's boring. So often I read sales collateral or newsletters or whatever, that is not compelling to read in the least. Worse still, the businesses behind them often *do* have something to say – a story to tell, or an interesting product, or an offer worth talking about. But, sadly, that's lost. No one, including paying customers, will wade deep enough into the text to work up much of an interest. For a business, boring writing is deadly (a slow, painful deadly).

That's why you should read this book. No, study it. Suze is a messiah to businesses who want to engage, not bore, their customers, even if writing comes as a bit of a chore. Writing is work. Good writing is even harder work. But Suze serves up the basics in a way that's easy to digest and apply to your own work.

Some people seem bred to write well. This book is for the rest of us – we who could use some step-by-step coaching in our writing to become, as Suze says, "brilliant".

Ann Handley
Chief Content Officer, Marketing Professionals
www.MarketingProfs.com
Co-author, *Content Rules*
http://www.contentrulesbook.com/

CONTENTS

INTRODUCTION

As you may already know, I've been a professional copywriter, screen and speech writer and latterly business/marketing journalist, for a long time. During those years I have been keeping my eyes and ears open to all forms of writing and allied disciplines like TV and conference production.

Result? I'm a walking encyclopedia of information about business writing!

In the early 2000s I decided to practise what I was preaching to clients about good online newsletters, and launch one of my own.

Tipz from Suze was what emerged and every other week I would send out some writing help to my list that grew to nearly 10,000 people in 47 countries.

After five great years I moved on from *Tipz* to my own website where I shared more of my experience and advice, and more recently to my lovely blogsite, *HowToWriteBetter.net*, where I've got even more room to share writing tips, masterclasses with other allied experts, plus a vast range of advice and hints from my own experience that readers find very helpful in their own writing.

Here, now, is a collection of the best of my discoveries and experiences – from a few years ago to very recent stuff – to provide you with just about everything you'll ever need to know on how to be brilliant at the business writing you need to do for success.

Suze

KEY TIPS

1. Before you write anything down **define not what you want to say, but what your message must achieve**. Keep that firmly in focus at all times and use it as the main goal for everything you write. Ask yourself, "does this concept/approach/clever headline/earnest mission statement really help the message achieve its objectives?" If the honest answer is no, alter it or rethink it completely.

2. Identify your target audience and get to know them very well. No matter how beautifully structured your message is, if it doesn't take into account the real circumstances and needs of the audience, it won't work. Align your message's objectives with these circumstances and needs.

3. Study the media you'll be using; **be aware of how people will receive your message** and where your message will be competing for their attention, use your common sense and creativity to make it stand out in the crowd. (Or if the crowd's too big, reconsider the choice of media if that's within your power.)

4. Now develop your message based on these issues, and **add in the final magic ingredient ... "what's in it for them?"** Successful business messages are always based on benefits for the target audience – either actual or implied. Ensure you know the difference between features and benefits, and how to convert features into benefits.

5. Research the way your target audience speak and communicate, and **phrase your message in their language** – which may not necessarily be yours. Avoid corporate pomposity and unnecessary jargon. Talk to "you", not some vague third party, and keep your English as simple as possible, especially when your message is going to people who originate from other cultures.

6. Traditional grammar and even spelling mostly have been thrown out of the window. However **there are still a few grammar rules you need to follow** if you don't want your message to look amateurish. Your knowledge of the audience and how they communicate will dictate your writing style to a large extent. Don't let catchwords, "internet-speak", emoticons, etc, obscure your message or its benefits.

7. Time pressures and the influence of the internet have made us into a world of browsers, even when we're reading brochures and other print. Unless it's very short, **organize your offline text so readers who are browsing get the key points very easily**. Always separate technical detail and other lengthy data from the main text so readers aren't obliged to plod through it unless they want to.

8. Never be tempted to transplant text written for print into an online environment. **Online text is as different from offline text as a PC screen is from paper**. Because reading from most screens is unfriendly, online text must be very short and crisp and must make it extremely easy for readers to absorb the key points. Don't let web designers talk you into flamboyant graphics that could inadvertently swamp your message.

9. When you give a speech, make sure you write it for yourself and your natural way of speaking – not your (or someone else's) idea of how an important business person should speak in public. Use a tape recorder to get an objective view of your voice, style, weaknesses and strengths. Keep sentences short with only one idea in each. Avoid telling jokes unless you're naturally funny. And rehearse, rehearse, rehearse.

10. If you think you may be out of your depth with a business writing project (e.g. a TV commercial, major direct marketing campaign, complex video or business theatre script) you're probably right – so **call in a professional writer**. Don't risk embarrassing yourself or your organization with an attempt that's amateurish. There's no shame in admitting you can't be an expert at everything!

THE BASICS

Tone of voice: write as people speak

TO WRITE AS PEOPLE SPEAK instantly knocks down barriers and makes your message seem friendlier, more plausible, and so more attractive. The internet has done a wonderful job of championing this style of writing and has made it pretty well mandatory. And now its influence has expanded that notion into printed text as well. Great!

Ah, easy though it sounds, achieving that fluency and simplicity of style isn't the piece of cake it appears to be. If for no other reason, most of us have had the "formal" brand of English brainwashed into our minds from schooldays and that's a hard one to eradicate.

So what's the answer?

Talk, don't write

Whether you're writing an email, a letter, a report, a proposal or even a brochure, forget the fact that you have to commit words to paper or screen. Instead imagine you're talking to a typical member of your audience.

You'll be amazed at how much easier the writing process becomes when you do this. That's because most of us are much more familiar with "talk" mode than we are with "write" mode, so in "talk" mode our thoughts flow more easily. It's useful to plan your "talk" around a structure of short bullet points, so you don't stray.

Then "talk" away. Ideally, record it, transcribe it, then edit and tidy it up. If you can't physically record it then imagine yourself talking through and write down those words, followed by editing and tidying.

It works. Even if you only have a few minutes to get the job done, it still works. And your business writing will be all the more effective for it.

Tone of voice: the "royal we"

The highly subjective "royal we" syndrome (so named as the British Queen Victoria supposedly said "we" instead of "I" when expressing her views, to stress her elevated royal status) is still seen all too often today. Favorite places for it to lurk are in corporate brochures, introductory website text, and DIY press releases.

Phrases like "we are proud to announce" or "we're in the unique position of leading the market in..." are far too subjective. They don't suggest anything in it for the reader and so act as a turnoff.

In today's business climate, "we" only interests your readers when they can see how "we" delivers a benefit to them. That means the "we" you use needs to be pro-active and wherever possible link to an actual or implied benefit for the audience.

"We felt sure you would want to be among the first to know that..." and "our low prices and good service have earned us our place as market leaders" offer an element of promise – something you want to share with the reader. That makes them feel that they're part of a dialogue, not listening to a lecture, so instantly they're more involved and more interested.

And this applies equally across the whole spectrum of writing styles and levels, from the snappiest radio commercial to the most formal of proposals.

Once you drop the "royal we" and become comfortable writing with the pro-active form of "we", you'll find you can blend it seamlessly into your organization's corporate image, brand and ethos. If anything, those will be enhanced by your increased focus on the audience in question, whoever they are.

Know your audience

It's easy to fall into the trap of thinking you know who your readers or viewers are. Unless you're one of them, you usually don't.

The point of getting to know your audience as well as you know yourself is to know how your message will be received in real life and what it will really mean to the recipients. If you know that, you can structure your message so that it will be as effective as possible, whether it's intended to sell, motivate, inform, entertain, instruct, or whatever.

Who are they?

To say your audience consists of pharmaceutical salespeople or car drivers or bank employees or newspaper editors tells you their titles, not who they are and where they're coming from. You need to know more than this. You need to understand their problems, the pressures they experience, the politics they may have to deal with, their financial circumstances, and how they view the world generally. It's only with that depth of knowledge that you will be able to formulate meaningful messages.

How technically literate are they?

The reason for needing to know this may seem very obvious, but, believe me, many messages sent out by companies are pitched too high or too low, because the communicators have made the wrong assumptions about the audience's prior knowledge of the subject matter. You need to find out the truth.

What does it feel like to be in their shoes?

Just because your boss thinks the region's newspaper editors are going to love the story of your company's recently awarded contract to supply tractor components to the government of Ecuador, they won't. Someone in your boss's shoes thinks it's a newsworthy event because he and the rest of the management team have spent six months working on it and it's going to up the company's share/stock value by a good 20%.

Someone in a newspaper editor's shoes sees it as just another bit of corporate PR that's of no interest to anyone other than a handful of his/her readers. Learn to empathize realistically.

Are these the people who will react to your message ultimately?

Sometimes people in your immediate audience are not in a position to make a decision single-handedly to act on your message – they may be the monkeys rather than the organ-grinders. There will be other people in the background – spouses, partners, colleagues, superiors, financial controllers or other unseen third parties – who may have some or even all of the say in the final decision.

Does your message have to work across a range of different audiences?

A tricky one, but here are three useful points to remember:

1. Whoever they are, they are all people and people have a lot in common whether they're growling teenagers with galloping hormones or elderly spinsters living in country cottages. If you create your message on the basis of appealing to human nature, you won't go far wrong.

2. There is usually one audience group that is more important than the others, and often it's possible to prioritize all the groups. You can then focus your message accordingly.

3. In my experience, writing for very diverse audience groups tends only to happen when the message is about something that has a very broad appeal anyway. Often the subject of your message is something very well known, or it's made/produced /devised/offered by a well-known organization. In this case you can depend on established brand values and not have to explain all that much to your audience, which allows your message to be simpler and more relevant to a wide spread of recipients.

Good quality research

Of course a lot of your research into your audience can, in theory, be done at your desk. Using a combination of your common sense, contacts and the internet, you can get hold of quite a lot of general information.

However, quality of information is important here. Even small nuances can make a huge difference to your understanding of the audience. And one thing desk research doesn't achieve is to uncover issues and problems that no-one likes to talk about. Yet often it's precisely these issues and problems – or at least your ignorance of them – that can dilute your message to an alarming degree.

Be a "mystery shopper"

There's a lot to be said for using "mystery shopper" techniques to research and get to know your audiences. Although some people might say it's dishonest to conceal your identity, the problem is people won't always be honest with you if you tell them who you really are.

That's especially true of rank-and-file staff in large organizations, if they think you're management. Many will tell you what they think you want to hear. Similarly consumers in stores and shopping malls will put up barriers, especially if you're walking around with a video camera crew or even an audio recorder.

You're far more likely to get the truth from staff in a large organization, say, if they think you're the person who's come in to fix the water cooler, or from shoppers if you're pushing a loaded cart in a supermarket and strike up a conversation with them while waiting to go through the checkout.

So how do you get people to open up and talk freely to you? You get them to talk about themselves.

How to "interview" people

There are very, very, few people in the industrialized world who actively will not warm to someone whom they believe is genuinely interested in them, their life, and their opinions. But members of your audience aren't idiots. If you're only pretending to be interested in them, they'll know. So you have to *be* interested. Really. And if you are, you'll get the results you want.

Here are some further tips on how to "interview" members of your audience:

- Remember news reporters' classic questioning structure of "who, what, where, when, how and why?" It may not be right to use it in every conversation you have, but it's a very good foundation.
- Be careful how you phrase your questions – always be tactful and polite. This is *not* hard-nosed journalism.
- Never ask a question that can be answered with a "yes" or a "no", because a yes or no answer won't help you much.
- Ask for opinions. People love to give their opinions.
- Always make your questions open-ended so they invite an answer, but be gentle – not, "Why do you hate the food in the canteen?" but, "People don't seem happy with the food from the canteen now – why do you think that is?"
- When asking a question, just ask one – don't include more than one key thought.
- When you've asked a question, shut up. Let the person speak. Don't interrupt or attempt to steer what they're saying.
- If they falter or hesitate on an important point, don't press them on it. Ask them something else, then return to your original point later on, remembering to ask the question in a different way so they don't realize it's the same point. You'll be surprised how well that can work.

- And when you've finished, thank them. They've helped you do your job better.

Features versus benefits

Anyone who has worked in sales knows that features are what something is, whereas benefits are what it does for you.

Successful sales writing – or even writing something to persuade others to agree with your point of view – depends to a large extent on converting all features into benefits for the target reader or viewer. That's based on the fact that most people don't want to change buying habits, actions, or even opinions unless there's "something in it for them".

So, by writing about benefits to them, you provide maximum motivation for them to change to what you want them to do.

But enough of this social psychology. How do we turn features into benefits and then make those benefits work for us?

Know the difference

First, let's be sure we're clear on how the difference between them works. Here are some typical product features (left) with their corresponding benefits (right):

AL-alloy metal frame with HK-147 PVC compound, polyurethane seat and back rest

You can relax in comfort – knowing its sturdy frame and durable seat back are not only comfortable, but they'll also last for many years

Fade-proof coating withstands sun and heat up to 35°C constant for 72 hours. Factory tested for efficacy

Looks good for years to come even in strong sun and sizzling summer temperatures, thanks to fade-proof, factory-tested coating

Delivered in flat pack with full assembly instructions. Pack suitable for long-term storage prior to assembly

Arrives in convenient pack ready to store for the winter... then assemble in minutes, ready for spring

Actually, there's a useful tool to help us turn a feature into a benefit. All you do is look at a feature and ask, "SO?"

In other words, "what's in it for the reader?"

I'll use some examples using my old friend Joe The Carpenter from my book, *Powerwriting*. Here we're creating a mailshot for a very good master carpenter who wants to consolidate his local business...

Joe the carpenter is highly skilled.
So... he knows what he is doing – if he claims this and isn't, he could get sued

He has 20 years' experience.
So... he won't waste your time or money because he knows what works and what doesn't

He's a local man, born and bred.
So... he's not likely to do a moonlight flit having half-completed your work, because people know where to find him

He's worked for some of the city's most respected residents, including the Mayor – some for many years.
So... he's reliable and trustworthy.

He has glowing testimonials from many of his customers who are prepared to say so if a new customer wants to ask them.

So... we have proof that he's doing something right; these days testimonials legally have to be true.

You can apply the "**So**" tool to almost any feature, whether tangible or intangible, and the answer to that question is what you need to use to create your benefits-led writing.

What if your writing project isn't about selling something tangible like garden furniture or carpentry, but a concept or other intangible message? In this case, you don't have features as such, but you do have objectives. Objectives usually are your objectives, not your audience's. So in effect they can be considered "features" and once again you need to turn them into benefits, by asking "so what's in it for them?" For example:

If you seek to:	The key benefit is that they:
Inform	Increase their knowledge
Sell something	Acquire and possibly pay for something that will enhance their life/job/sex appeal/whatever
Train	Improve their skills and abilities so they are better at what they do

Rebuke	Learn how to overcome the difficulty and become better at their job
Complain	Can give even better service next time
Entertain	Enjoy themselves!
Calm	Be placated, soothed, and stop worrying
Sympathize	Know that you support them when they have a problem
Reassure	Can be confident in themselves and in you/your organization
Energize	Believe they're free to be more optimistic
Motivate	Believe that it's well worth their while to put in greater effort
Uplift	Feel good about what they're doing and feel inspired to do it even better

One problem you can get with benefits: too many of them

Sometimes in a business communication project you'll be dealing with what appear to be dozens of features which turn into at least several benefits. Usually that is an illusion, because even an apparently unrelated selection of benefits will probably have a common denominator. And it's the common denominator – the "umbrella" benefit – that's going to grab your audience's interest. Not a shopping list of different, lesser benefits.

Lots of benefits amount to just that – lots of benefits, which have a way of diluting each other's impact. One key "umbrella" benefit, though, not only gets attention – it also provides a central focus for what your message is all about. To find your "umbrella" benefit, ask yourself, "so what do all these benefits actually boil down to? What's the bottom line benefit?"

In the case of Joe The Carpenter, you could probably approach it in more than one way. But I think his bottom line benefit is:

Joe the carpenter gives you high-quality carpentry you can really rely on, to care for your home.

OK. What if, as sometimes happens, there are no obvious benefits to the reader?

For example, if your key message is this: "I need more money to finance my business and I want to borrow it from you." Here you need to look a bit harder, but usually it's still possible to drum up something.

If you use "Request for further finance" as the subject heading in a letter or e-mail to the finance company then it's clear there is absolutely nothing in it for them, so you'd better be a good customer and regular payer to stand a chance.

However, what about "Capital required to launch sought-after new product"? Or even a play on the heartstrings with "Request for further funding to secure company's future and employees' jobs"? Both of those offer the reader something, at least, which is always better than nothing at all.

When in doubt, think positive!

Grammar

Now that the mass media with its "newspeak" vocabulary has been part of our lives for several generations, we really can't afford to be pompous about spelling and grammar any more. Even the stuffiest of academics has had to admit that stiffly formal writing is not clever, it's boring. They may look down their elegant, aquiline noses at the language of popular tabloid newspapers, FMCG advertising and, more recently, the Internet, but that's the language nearly everyone speaks today.

I won't bore you with my theories on why that has happened, but the bottom line is that English as a language has become simpler and less complex than it was 100 years ago. And quite right too. I've never understood why some people get so uppity about the fact that a language has evolved. Well, you and I haven't got time to mourn the relegation of Shakespearean English to books and the stage, even if we want to. We've got work to do here and now, and these days we write as we speak.

It's OK to write as people speak

"Writing as people speak" is not an excuse to be lazy or ungrammatical. It's a faster and more efficient way of putting across ideas and communicating messages.

And because you don't have the formality of old-fashioned "grammatically correct" syntax, clauses, long adjectives and everything else to hide behind, your message is standing out there all by itself. So it's got to be strong enough to hold its own without the support that old-fashioned writing often gives to less-than-strong messages.

Having said that old-fashioned writing with perfect grammar and syntax and spelling etc can be forgotten, am I saying that today we can all write what we like in the way that we like? Well yes, but wait a minute.

Rather like with golf or poker, with writing you really should know what the rules are before you can benefit from breaking them. Now, I'm not going to launch into a lesson in English grammar here because that would be insulting your intelligence and education. It would also be intensely boring.

The little goofs let you down

What you really do need to avoid is not the blatant, deliberate thumbing of the nose at grammatical correctness such as that found in consumer advertising campaigns, but the piffling little mistakes you see in some business communication which are simply the result of ignorance and carelessness.

These are the goofs that separate the professionals from the amateurs. It's the body copy that talks about "you" in the same sentence as "them" when referring to the same person. It's the long-winded sentence in a business letter or e-mail that has so many dangling participles you could decorate a Christmas tree with them. It's the absence of an apostrophe when we're talking about "it is" and the inclusion of an apostrophe when we're talking about something belonging to "it."

(And in the UK at least, it's the inclusion of an adverb between the two halves of an infinitive... many Brits still cringe when they hear the *Startrek* line of "to boldly go..." But in the USA no-one seems to mind. Ah, *vive la différence*.)

If you challenge grammar rules, be bold

These small slips and goofs in grammar, punctuation and syntax really do cheapen people's written material and they drop the writer's credibility right into the doo-doo. But the bold gestures... the one-word sentence, the verbless sentence, the folkloric use of slang and so-on... these are so obvious that no-one is going to think they are oversights.

This makes them acceptable – even effective.

If you take a look at some of the top-end consumer advertising that I so enjoy snarling at most of the time, you'll see how such deliberate, bold grammatical mistakes not only work well, but also manage to make the advertising look classy and svelte. The secret of success here is the intelligent and measured use of poor grammar, and that's something professional copywriters are very good at.

For well-meaning amateurs, however, remember that there's only a fine line between the slick and the sloppy and it takes experience and expertise to keep everything on the slick side. It's a lot safer to stay away from the borderline so, if you want to play the brinkmanship game, you have been warned...

Spelling

Accurate spelling is something I value. I know that sounds very old-fashioned in the light of modern day text messaging and online shortcuts and abbreviations, but like most things there are good reasons behind what sometimes appears like unnecessary rule-following. In the case of good spelling, I believe the reason is to maintain uniformity, which leads to accuracy.

The other reason why some people see good spelling as desirable is to demonstrate the writer's level of education and literacy, but I'm not sure if this is a particularly accurate gauge. One of the worst spellers I've ever known was a doctor who could write out prescriptions using perfect 20-letter pharmaceutical terms but couldn't write a postcard to his mother without six or seven goofs in it. The other atrocious speller I know is a brilliant mathematician and is definitely not dyslexic.

Spell checkers are OK, but not perfect

Most word processing software includes some sort of spelling checker device and these are helpful, but not infallible. They will pick up typos and glaring mistakes but, being machines, are far too logical to cope with the insanity of the English language and can't deal with homophones or wrong words that are spelled right or apostrophes appearing in the wrong place.

Many word processing packages also incorporate grammar/syntax nannies, rather like mine which sticks a disapproving green line under most of my work. I ignore it. Finally, most word processing packages give you the option to select UK or USA spellings, which leads us directly into another can of worms.

Which English spellings – UK or US?

Many people ask me how text should be spelled for international English language communication. My answer is I don't know. Possibly you should spell according to the organization's country of origin – where its headquarters and roots are. But that gets blown straight out of the water if the company's origins are a small distillery in the Highlands of Scotland which has now been supplemented by a multi-million dollar manufacturing and distribution operation incorporating 24 huge factory/warehouse sites coast to coast in the United States.

Possibly, then, you should spell according to the country in which the largest amount of the organization's business is done, but with hierarchies being what they are this may not work out evenly either. Probably, though, if we wait for a while the internet will solve the problem because, through its aggressive internationalism, English language spellings will become standardized everywhere.

And, because the US has the rest of us by the short hairs on the internet, there are no prizes for guessing which type of English we'll standardize to. Although the mere thought of it will make most British-speak purists burst into tears, I must say I'm looking forward to the day when I can write out a "check" in the UK for new "tires" on my car and then go home and watch a good "program" on TV.

So what can you do to improve your spelling?

In the first instance, consult your spellchecker and then be sure to human check any ambiguous elements. Also, use the Thesaurus facility if you're unsure how to spell a particular word: enter a simpler synonym that you can spell and your other word should come up.

Alternatively, at the risk of sounding like my usual low-tech self, I would say use a dictionary. Despite being paper-based, a dictionary is often the faster way to find a word.

A bit of (clean) fun to finish

"Aoccdrnig to a rscheearch at Cmabrigde Uinervtisy, it deosn't mttaer in waht oredr the ltteers in a wrod are, the olny iprmoetnt tihng is taht the frist and lsat ltteer be at the rghit pclae. The rset can be a toatl mses and you can sitll raed it wouthit porbelm. Tihs is bcuseae the huamn mnid deos not raed ervey lteter by istlef, but the wrod as a wlohe."

Yes, you got it:

"According to a researcher (sic) at Cambridge University, it doesn't matter in what order the letters in a word are, the only important thing is that the first and last letter be at the right place. The rest can be a total mess and you can still read it without problem. This is because the human mind does not read every letter by itself but the word as a whole."

So it seems as long as the first and last letters of a word are correct, our eyes/brains are programmed to understand it. Does this blow the whole need for good spelling out of the water?

Punctuation

The fuss generated a few years ago by Lynne Truss's book, *Eats Shoots and Leaves: the zero tolerance approach to punctuation,* brought this topic into focus. From the way everyone was talking when the book came out, you'd think punctuation was a whole new, previously unappreciated art form that could light up all our lives.

In the cold light of the business day, though, punctuation is not much more than a set of tools we use to fine tune our writing -- nothing more romantic than that.

You've probably noticed that it tends to split into two separate categories:

1. Punctuation that affects the meaning of what you write (so it's worth getting right)
2. Punctuation that doesn't really affect the meaning of what you write (but irritates some people if you get it wrong)

Beyond that, also there are variations in punctuation rules from one English language culture to the next. Most of those, I would say, fall into category two.

So let's take a look at the topic from the non-literary, business-only viewpoint. Please note these are my opinions only and I'm no English graduate – only a realist – so feel free to disagree!

Punctuation that affects the meaning of what you write (so it's worth getting right)

APOSTROPHE

This is probably the most misunderstood punctuation element of them all. Time and time again I see examples of the apostrophe incorrectly used and I think, "well, if I can get them right on the strength of mere high school /secondary school English, why can't they?" Apostrophes are easy. Here's how:

The apostrophe is used in three main ways:

1. To make a noun possessive: Suze's, the children's, everyone's. And if it has an "s" at the end of the original noun, then the apostrophe goes after that: cheeses', helpers', mothers', etc.

2. To show you've left something out and/or contracted two words: don't, won't, she'll, he'd, etc; and most importantly, "it's" as in the contraction of "it is".

3. To indicate plurals of some lower case letters, but only a few, as in "mind your p's and q's".

The apostrophe is *not* used to accompany possessive pronouns or for noun plurals, including acronyms and well-known abbreviations.

So you *do not* need an apostrophe in examples like "his", "yours", "hers", "its" (aha, that's why!), etc

Similarly you *do not* need an apostrophe to make plurals out of things like "the 1970s", "Ipods", "PCs" etc

COMMA

Here's another really useful punctuation mark. Commas split thought processes after introductory

1. words,
2. phrases, or
3. clauses,

particularly where there would be a pause in natural speech.

Here is an example of each:

1. However, I'm delighted to say that...
2. From the employee's perspective, I can see we need to...
3. Looking at it from the employee's perspective, I can see we need to...

SEMI COLON

This creates a more dramatic pause, usually to link two clauses if you don't want to use a verbal link like "and" or "but".

With verbal link:
I want to go to the wine bar, but I have work to do here.

Without verbal link:
I want to go to the wine bar; I have work to do here, however.

You also use semi colons to create a list when any of the items concerned contain punctuation of their own, like commas – for example:

Apples, pears and oranges; tomatoes, bell peppers and lemons; broccoli, cabbage and green beans.

BULLET POINTS

In modern business writing, especially for online purposes, it's usually better to use bullet points to form a list, because they're easier to follow both verbally and visually. Generally you should use them for lists of three or more points, and probably for no more than about ten without some sort of break.

COLON

This creates an even more definitive pause. It's most frequently used after a complete (short) statement so you can introduce one or more directly related ideas. If they come in list form you may want to use semi colons to separate the list entries that follow.

For example:
The following people were instrumental in helping us achieve our goals: John Doe, senior chemist; Mary Jones, technical manager; Joe Bloggs, technical advisor; Jane Smith, liaison officer.

Don't forget, too, that colons form an essential part of timings (e.g. 05:00 hours, 6:00 p.m.).

PERIOD/FULL STOP
Need I say more? Well, yes. Be sure you use this punctuation mark often enough. Long sentences in contemporary business communications tend to wander and obscure meaning. Shorter sentences are punchier, better understood, and far more powerful.

PARENTHESES/BRACKETS
Parentheses section off extra thoughts that, although not critical, are still relevant to a sentence, e.g.:

I wondered if the old homestead (which had been built in the 19th century) would withstand this modern onslaught of renovation.

DASH
To an extent, dashes perform the same function as parentheses, for example:

I wondered if the old homestead – which had been built in the 19th century – would withstand this modern onslaught of renovation. They also can be used in the same way as a colon, e.g.:

I wondered if the old homestead would withstand this modern onslaught of renovation – having been built in the 19th century, it might not have been strong enough.

QUOTATION MARKS/INVERTED COMMAS

These marks show direct quotations. Whether other punctuation marks, like commas, periods/full stops, colons and semi colons, go inside or outside the quote marks depends on where you went to school! However today the generally accepted rule is that if whatever goes between those marks consists of a complete sentence on its own, the punctuation goes inside the marks. If the content is just a few words or otherwise *not* a complete sentence, the punctuation goes after the closing mark/inverted comma.

Quote marks also indicate words you want to pull out to suggest irony or some other quirk, but should not be overused.

In an advertising or promotional context, some people feel that to put quote marks around a statement will make readers believe it has been said by some authoritative person and therefore deserves to be taken seriously.

Well, I know that can work when you're advertising a fairly low-level product to a certain mass-market level. But believe me, if you operate in the higher echelons of business-to-business communications, forget that one. If you want it to be believed, make sure you attribute it to its genuine originator.

Punctuation that doesn't really affect the meaning of what you write (but irritates some people if you get it wrong)

HYPHEN

Hyphens are used to join two words into one compound word, e.g. well-known, eighty-three, semi-skilled. You also should hyphenate words with some prefixes and suffixes like ex-wife, mid-1970s, self-interested, chairman-elect.

EXCLAMATION MARK

People often tend to overuse the exclamation mark, which weakens its impact. I'm guilty of this. Often I'll compose an email to someone, then go back and edit out all but one or two of the "screamers". Too many of these cheapen your writing, even if it is intended to be light-hearted.

LEADER DOTS...

Another "guilty" from Suze... see? You can use these instead of parentheses or dashes, but they are frowned upon by some people. To be safe, it's better to use them sparingly or not at all.

UNDERLINING

Underlining is a common way to emphasize text, but be very careful about using it in text that is intended to be used online. Here, an underlined word or words in an email or web text can represent a link. It's best to use the **bold** facility for emphasis.

ITALICS

Another means of emphasizing text. Online, try to avoid using it unless your font is large, because italics are not easy to read from a screen. Traditionally they're used to show the title of something like a play (e.g. *Hamlet, The Merchant of Venice*), newspaper, magazine or journal (*The Sun, New York Times*), and also some foreign words (e.g. *haute cuisine, schadenfreude*).

SLASH/OBLIQUE

This is often used to represent and, or, or and/or. Use it sparingly online as it can be visually confusing.

Mechanics

Many people shrug off the mechanical side of writing as irrelevant or, at most, unimportant.

But even to hardened old campaigners like me, how – and to a lesser extent where – you physically record your words does make a difference to their ultimate quality.

Mind you, in my job you learn how to write wonderful words in all sorts of undesirable environments. Many times I have written and edited complex speeches on a laptop while sitting (sometimes squatting if there are no spare chairs) backstage of a conference set while electricians, carpenters and riggers haul cables and build things all around me.

That old line about necessity being the mother of invention is very true. It's surprising how you can galvanize your thinking into action despite maniacal circumstances, when the alternative is a disappointed or worse, irate client.

The right environment

Ideally you should try to do your writing in as quiet and comfortable surroundings as possible. Your own home may seem ideal, but be careful. Unless you're very disciplined, working at home can be even more distracting than at your usual workplace (unless that's in your home, of course...).

If I have to concentrate particularly hard on a writing task, I find it does help to get away from my usual working environment and go somewhere where I'm not reminded of the other jobs and activities waiting to be done.

In my case, my office is a room in my house. So usually I'll take a pen and notepad and go sit at the table in my dining room. In an external office environment, you could perhaps borrow an empty meeting room, or even an absent colleague's office. You might be surrounded by their daily distractions, but they won't affect you as much as your own do.

Getting the words down

One of the biggest barriers that restricts the flow of your words – if you use a computer to write, and most people do – is lack of keyboard skills.

Just because you know how to use a computer does not necessarily mean you have learned to use more than two fingers on the *qwerty* keyboard. And if you need to write a lot of text it's well worth taking a course in touch typing, or even text management. You'll be amazed at how much faster and more pleasantly you can record your words when you use both thumbs and all eight fingers while keeping your eyes on the screen.

There are various ways of learning how to touch type, from attending a course at a local adult education college, to CD-ROMs to software packs you install in your computer.

If you Google the phrase "touch typing" you'll find thousands of companies offering training in touch typing via a range of different delivery media. Some of those would be well worth a browse.

Dictation

I have never succeeded in dictating anything other than garbage into these systems and I'm not the only writer who feels that way. However many famous authors dictate their work into audio recording devices, to be transcribed by long-suffering secretaries, and for them it works well.

Apparently the late Dame Barbara Cartland, the famous British romantic novelist, dictated every one of her books with an average output of one complete novel every two weeks. No-one knows how much editing had to be done to them and by whom. But with 723 books published in her lifetime of 98 years and another 160 unpublished titles still being released, she must have been doing something right.

Most business people who have the experience of dictating business letters should be able to dictate other simple writing tasks with the same efficiency. But realistically, audio recorders are more useful as information gathering tools from which you can transcribe the good stuff and incorporate it into your written text.

Voice recognition systems

Many people swear by these gizmos and in theory they speed up the creative process by removing the need for transcription. I find them horribly distracting, but that's probably because I'm a boring old Luddite. You may totally disagree.

Before investing time and money into an elaborate voice recognition system, in your shoes I would, if possible, try one out over a period of time and see if it really is as much of a time saver as all that. Unless you're very good at verbalizing your thoughts, you may find it takes longer to re-edit everything the system records than it would had you typed it all in the first place.

Making your case

How to make your case in a piece of business communication is about the same length as that proverbial piece of string, because the variation from a six-word mobile text advertisement at one end of the scale, to a 60-page business plan at the other doesn't involve too many similarities, as you know. So it's not something that easily fits into a formula.

However for the formula-lovers among us, I've done my best, and here it is.

Most of the time you can look at making your case through this trio of "...tions".

- No**tion**
- Informa**tion**
- Ac**tion**

You begin with a **notion** (statement of fact and/or proposition plus key benefit to audience, why you are reading/watching/listening to this and why you should continue to the end, what this is and what's in it for you)...

...which you need to support immediately with **information** (why your notion is important, how the benefit has been made possible, why the notion is more important than/more beneficial than what other organizations do)...

...and eventually, whether after each notion or after a group of notions, you introduce **action** (what the anticipated outcome is, what will happen next, what you need to do next, and a brief reprise of why).

The three "tions" pretty much cover all

As I said, there are huge variations depending on the subject matter, the message and the media, but as a rough guide I believe the three "tions" should be treated as equally important. Obviously that doesn't mean measuring it out in equal numbers of words – only equal importance in the "weight" you allocate to them.

Many examples of corporate communication don't work because one of the "tions" has assumed a far greater role than the other two. This is especially true of the classic "corporate" brochure where there are pages and pages about the organization and what it does and how it does it (information) but nothing is said about what it's doing in the reader's hands in the first place (no notion).

Ask yourself these questions

Another helpful tool in making your case is to ask yourself this list of key questions, having first cast yourself in the role of the audience. Then, ensure that what you write answers those questions, in the same order. This is the basis of any reasoned argument, really. You can also see how it works in a completely different context by reading copy in press advertisements or direct mail, and in a miniaturized version in many TV commercials or online ads. In a more restrained way you'll see it working in editorial pieces and even medical or academic papers and theses.

Why am I receiving this communication from you? (The message in a nutshell, the main notion, a little information to support it, and a strong hint of required action.)

So what's the problem? (Information about why the notion is valid, what has led up to it, the issues your notion addresses.)

What else should I know about? (Related sub-notions that add relevance, information to support them.)

And you have the solution? (Main notion again in more detail, supported by information on how it will work in practice.)

What happens next? (Action – try to state why they should do what you say, or why the next steps will make an improvement, etc, so the action offers some kind of reward – something "in it for them." Otherwise it will just read/sound like instructions or unsubstantiated predictions.)

Editing

The *Concise Oxford Dictionary* defines the word "edit" as "...set in order for publication..." In practice, editing can mean anything from a quick tidy-up of spelling and grammatical goofs, to a savage massacre that reduces a piece to a few clipped sentences.

Some people (usually editors!) believe that good editing of a piece of text is as important as the initial writing of it. I think that's true in instances where the original text is a mess for whatever reason – over-written, repetitive, long-winded, pompous, full of jargon, etc.

However if you structure your writing properly in the first place and write appropriately for the topic and audience concerned, extensive editing shouldn't be necessary.

I believe you need to strike a happy medium with editing. Tighten your text up, by all means, but don't throttle it to death, or it will lose its personality.

Editing criteria

The first part of the editing process acts like a final reality check on your writing. Here you need to adapt the five key elements of the **MAMBA**™ structure in my eBook, The MAMBA Way To Make Your Words Sell.

M is for mission. Does the piece really achieve what I set out to achieve – not merely get over what I want to say?

A is for audience. Have I really understood the audience I'm writing for and does this text connect with their needs and drives?

M is for media. Does this text (or script) work well for its chosen medium? E.g., if it's web text, is it short, snappy and scannable? If it's for spoken speech, does it sound natural when I read it aloud?

B is for benefits. If my writing needs to bring about some sort of change in the audience's behavior or perception, have I supplied them with sufficient reason to change? Have I made clear what's in it for them?

A is for articulation. Have I chosen the right style and tone of voice to articulate my message? Am I sure the audience will understand every word?

If the answer is "yes" to all those points and your word count is right for the space/time concerned, then you're unlikely to need much editing. If you answer "no" to one or more points, see if you can rectify the problem with a few small changes. If you can't, though, you may find it easier overall to start again with a complete rethink.

The same applies if your text turns out to be way too long.

Shortening your text

I've always found that if I need to shorten my text by more than a bit I have to start removing content, and that's where the balance can go seriously wrong.

If you need to reduce the length of a piece by more than about 20%, you'll do better to re-craft it from scratch – editing your thinking, rather than editing your words. That way your final piece of work will hang together far more effectively than if it's just a "shadow of its former self".

Structure

This is a pruning process and apart from the thorns is similar to pruning roses. Yes, you need to be quite radical at times in order to strip out dead wood and irrelevant suckers. But if you strip out too much you'll end up depleting the flowering potential, or even killing the plant.

First, satisfy yourself that your message flows in the correct order. Essentially, follow the old principle of "a beginning, a middle, and an end":

- Does it start by identifying clearly the key point of the piece?
- Does it provide convincing and accurate substantiation?
- Does it conclude and summarize the main issue?
- If relevant, is there a strong call to action?

Style

Style will depend to a large extent on the audience you're writing to, but there are a few common denominators that apply pretty much across the board:

- Take out any adjectives and adverbs that don't work genuinely hard
- Remove repetitive words, phrases and sentences
- Make sure each sentence flows logically into the next
- Make sure paragraphs and sections flow in logical sequence too
- Where appropriate use sub-headings to make text more readable and scannable
- Run a final spell check and double check homophones, etc, yourself

Edit from screen or printed page?

No matter how satisfied I can be with a piece of writing on screen, once I print it out I nearly always find further improvements to be made.

I know other professional writers experience the same thing, but it could also be an age-related issue. Old goats like me who grew up with typewriters had our grounding with paper-based writing. That could be why we can "see" our work more easily that way.

On the other hand, my son does his university assignments on a laptop and when he's editing and checking, he "sees" no difference between screen and paper.

Personal preference prevails!

Others' opinions

If you're not a professional writer (and even if you are) it sometimes helps to show your work to someone else and ask their view. But be careful. People will often go to ridiculous lengths to find something in your writing to criticize, just because they feel it's expected of them.

If you want a balanced opinion from a colleague/friend/family member/etc, don't hand them your writing and say, "What do you think of this?" That suggests you're expecting them to be critical.

Instead, say you'd like them to imagine they're the recipient of your writing. Recap to them the basis of your message – what you want and/or need to achieve with this piece of writing. Then ask them if, as the recipient, they would go along with your message.

With this approach you almost certainly will get more than a "yes" or a "no." And if there are any negatives you can ask why. The answers will be less about your writing than about your thinking in the written piece, which is probably where it will have gone wrong anyway.

Others' editing

Sometimes your writing will have to be edited by others – e.g. senior colleagues – whether you like it or not.

If this happens, do not let it go to its final destination before you've had another good look at it. Even if the other people have tried to be careful in editing your work, the fact that they didn't create it to begin with means they're not as in tune with it as you are.

If someone has made a change that really is nonsensical, change it back again, even if that someone was your boss. In the end, you're probably the one who will get into trouble if the mistake gets through, so look after your own interests. (And blame me if it goes wrong!)

Some last words on editing...

Montréal based online copywriter Nick Usborne recommends this, and I agree totally! You can read more about Nick here: *http://www.nickusborne.com*

> *"...cross out the first paragraph and start reading from paragraph two instead. What you'll often find is that very little is lost by scratching those first few lines... How come? Because the writer was warming up. Lots of writers, myself included, throw a few words at the page just to get started. The experienced writer will then go back and cut away the 'warm up' stage."*

And from me...

Once you've finished your final text, leave it for a while, then go back and take another look. No matter how wonderful you think it is, you'll always find something to tidy up or improve on after you've had a good night's sleep or even a walk around the office and a quick cup of coffee.

Don't start editing until you've finished writing the whole first draft. If you try to fiddle with your work as you go along you'll lose the momentum of your thinking.

Writer's block

Writer's block is no artsy cliché – it can be a real pain that holds you up for expensive hours. The blank screen or piece of paper has terrified even famous authors for generations and we poor business mortals suffer just as badly.

Unlike the famous authors of old, we usually haven't got time to seek inspiration through bacchanalian debauchery or an uplifting stroll amongst "a host of golden daffodils". However there are a few tricks we can use and they work for pretty well everything from an email to a brochure or business proposal.

Don't try to get it right first time

One of the mistakes we all make is that we try to get it right first time. No matter how much we might experiment with a message or concept in our minds, the first time we commit that to screen or paper, by golly it's got to be perfect. This is foolish, because it steers you straight into writer's block.

There is no need to practise economy if you're using a computer to write. Screen space is available on a pretty well limitless basis and all it costs you is the power bill (and then only if you're self-employed). Even if you use paper, you'll still need to write an awful lot before you've used up a fraction of a tree's worth. So forget perfect and get writing.

Start by writing around the point, not straight to it

By that I mean start by writing down anything at all. If you don't yet feel confident about writing down your message, don't try. Instead write **about** your message. What you want it to achieve. What you should remember to tell your audience about it. How it will benefit your audience to do what you're suggesting.

This removes the writer's block because now you're not exposing your vulnerable soft underbelly directly to that frightening foe called "audience". For the moment you're just writing notes to yourself which normally doesn't cause a block problem. However, this writing is still very productive. You're working through the message development process by writing down its strong points and most important of all, what's in it for your audience.

Keep that flow going to express the first version of your message

Once your writing is jogging along nicely it's time to start aiming for the actual message you'll use. But once again, don't risk hitting writer's block by attempting to tackle this head-on. Take a verbal detour and go around the longer, gentler way.

Simply continue writing, but change direction as you go. It doesn't matter how long-winded it is, because you're going to edit it later. Just narrow your focus on what you need to convey and write that up in as many words as you want. Think about your target audience while you're writing. Imagine you're sitting next to them in a bar or on a plane. Imagine you're chatting with them casually and informally – sharing what's on your mind.

It won't be perfect. In fact it may even be something like this...

The instrument in question is constructed from lightweight wood the interior of which houses a cylindrical core of carbon. It is necessary to sharpen the surrounding wood at the end of this instrument in order to obtain a conical point and expose the carbon core appropriately. Once this preparatory start-up sequence has been implemented the structure involved enables the object to be held in the dominant hand and, through the application of the correct degree of pressure and suitable movement of hand and arm, the carbon point will convey an image upon the piece of paper placed directly beneath it. At this time it is not a meaningful proposition for the foregoing technique to be demonstrated in a live situation, due to the hardware's non-permanent redistribution to a remote location.

Now edit hard and you get a final message that works

Look at what you've written and say to yourself, "OK, that's all fine and dandy, but what do I really mean?" This is where you get down to business. Chop-chop time.

In most cases, you'll dump all the security-blanket jargon, business-ese and excessive trimmings. That's stuff we tend to hide behind when we're unsure of what we really want to say. Now it's all there under your nose, though, it's easy to see where you've over-worded and replace that with concise, unfancy English your audience can identify with.

You'll also remove all superfluous information and leave only the facts your audience cares about. This means streamlining the issues, focusing those on the audience, promoting the benefits and developing it all around key points. You don't have to explain every last detail. Direct is beautiful.

Something like this, perhaps...

I'm talking about a pencil. It's made of wood with some carbon inside it. If you sharpen one end, you can write with it. Right now I can't show you how it works because I've mislaid it.

So when writer's block strikes, remember:

1. Don't try to get it right first time
2. Start by writing around the point, not straight to it
3. Keep that flow going to express the first version of your message
4. Now edit hard and you get a final message that works

Writing for the Web

How online writing styles can improve offline writing

AFTER ALL THE AGONIES WE suffered some years ago when people tried to make offline text work online, we've finally turned the tables. Now we can borrow back a number of online writing concepts and use them to sharpen up whatever paper-based marketing communications we still write.

Remember how early website text could make you cringe? Squinting at all 2000 solidly crammed words so obviously lifted straight from an equally cringe-making corporate brochure? Peering at that fat, uniformly gray column of garbage scrolling hypnotically up through the browser window?

Well, nearly all of that went some years ago to the Great Delete Tab in the sky, thanks to people like Jakob Nielsen (and many others) who showed us how to get real and write for the web as it should be done.

Now, though, there's evidence that Dr Nielsen's chickens are coming home to roost back in the old offline barn.

First of all, there's a cosmetic trend for online notions to powder the nose of paper-based communication... web and email jargon, smiley faces, text abbreviations (U h8 txt 2?) and more are turning up in printed material every day.

More usefully, many of us who write for a living are applying some online writing techniques and approaches to our offline work, too. In fact the very "fashionableness" of all things online has given us the excuse we needed to clear out a lot of the awful old junk that's been cluttering up some clients' offline text for years.

1. It's essential to have clear objectives

Any piece of online communication that doesn't have clear-cut objectives comes over as chinless and indecisive. Many printed documents have got away with being chinless and indecisive in the past, but no more – possibly due, in part, to online influences. If they're going to be taken seriously today, printed comms need clear objectives too – driven by what you want to achieve, not just what you want to say.

2. People often prefer to scan and go back to get detail later

Although online text has championed scanning, people have been scanning offline text like brochure copy since long before the www came to be. Online, to facilitate scanning we break up text with highlighting, bold type and crossheads which enable readers to get the gist of our message in a few seconds. Paper-based messages can be improved dramatically when given the same treatment.

3. People do not always read in a linear fashion

We don't expect people to view our website pages in any particular sequence. This is not new. For years people have been leafing through brochures starting at the back, skipping to the front, dipping into the middle and back again. Longish offline content benefits greatly from being organized on a non-linear basis to cater equally for the linear readers and the grasshoppers.

4. Not everyone needs or wants the technical stuff

Even with high-tech business, we often put the techie details in their own little cubby-hole on a website, or in a downloadable PDF file. That way they're there for those who are interested but don't obscure the main marketing messages. Offline messages gain in the same way, when you box off technical data or append it to the back of a document.

5. Visual clutter confuses readers

In the same way that people loathe website home pages that bristle with shouting headlines and graphics and other grinning gargoyles, they hate cluttered print and press ads that shriek "busy, busy". If it's hard to find your message in amongst garish junk, online or offline, they'll just flip or click over to your competitors' information.

6. BS is boring

Everyone sees through hype now. The online environment makes it look even sillier than ever. Readers of any marketing communication, online or off, expect your writing to talk directly to them, as one human being speaks to another. If you wouldn't insult a customer by using boastful, pompous hype face-to-face and online, why do it offline?

7. Complex thinking doesn't work

Although long copy often works online, the writing style itself needs to be very economical and uncomplicated. Every word has to earn its keep. Sentences and paragraphs should be short and free from convoluted notions. And that's an approach that also works wonders to clarify and enliven text for brochures, print newsletters, and other longer marketing communications.

8. Lists in the form of long sentences don't get read

Online, if you have more than two or three items to list you're advised to create bullets, rather than run them together in a long sentence. If that makes them quicker to absorb online, think what a beneficial effect it can have on lists in offline text.

9. Headlines and crossheads must be relevant, not cutesy-clever

In the online environment these lines often have to stand alone – e.g. as email subject lines – so must be directly relevant. Also, they must appeal to the search engines which certainly have no time for anything other than straight talking. Although abstract headlines are acceptable in some press ads, in longer offline text the headlines are what people latch on to while scanning. This means they also have to be directly relevant, so they're instantly understood.

10. Cut the c*ap and get to the point

Not only do online comms demand uncluttered information, but also relevant information. People haven't got time to wait 10 minutes while your incredibly creative animation downloads, and equally they haven't time to figure out the meaning of a literary quote over an arty picture when they're in a hurry to find out about your diesel generators. In our high-speed business culture, direct is beautiful.

Emails

Learn about etiquette (or "netiquette") for writing emails

There are loads of good reference websites and books about the internet which will tell you the basics. I know it might seem a bit precious to attach so much importance to social niceties when the internet is basically very informal. However, whether we like it or not, many people do take online etiquette very seriously. So if you're writing emails for business, you should assume that your recipient may well be one of those...

Avoid being emotional and/or hasty

Never send and preferably don't even try to write an email if you're angry, upset, drunk, or otherwise not in total control.

If you have a heated conversation with someone on the telephone you can sometimes fudge things over. But with emails, once you hit "send", whatever you've written is there, carved in tablets of stone, for as long as the recipient wants to glare at it. The old adage about "counting to ten" before responding couldn't be more true here. Only send angry emails if you can handle, or really don't care about, the recipient's resultant feelings!

Timing

One thing that you may not think of is that it can be useful to consider carefully the time you send your emails.

To begin with it's always a good idea to avoid sending emails that coincide with the Monday morning rush and Friday afternoon lethargy. In addition, I've occasionally found that emails sent to companies over the weekend end up getting lost in cyberspace. And, on a rather more subtle level, if your recipients see that you're sending emails on a Sunday morning or late at night, they may feel they can interrupt you for a business talk at the same times. Although you may think it's cool to impress a client that you work all hours, your partner won't when the same client calls you on the phone at midnight.

Attachments

Because almost everyone at some time or another has been infected with a computer virus, people are understandably wary of attachments.

I never send attachments to anyone I don't know very well and, equally, never open attachments unless they're from people I know well. And then some contemporary viruses and worms clone themselves on to genuine email names and addresses, so even an email purporting to be from someone you know might just be infected. When in doubt append text to the body of your email message, or contact the recipient beforehand and make sure they're happy to receive it as an attachment.

Layout

Layout of emails is something few people pay attention to, especially if their system uses text only.

However, even with simple text a sensible layout can make the whole thing more readable. Above all, you should avoid writing emails that sprawl all the way across the screen. Those are very hard to read and to be able to see everything properly as text, your reader may have to fiddle about changing fonts. The safest format to use consists of lines no more than 65 characters long. That fits, works everywhere and makes the email much easier on the eye.

Online writing

Online writing has to be kept concise and clear, largely because the screen can be an unfriendly reading medium for most people's eyes – especially when they're reading from mobile devices.

If only for that reason, the KISS principle (Keep It Short and Simple) is useful. With emails you need to get straight to the point and keep to it. Someone who receives dozens of emails a day doesn't have time to wade through a lot of preamble. Someone who is reading off a screen the size of playing card doesn't need to wade through a lot of verbiage, either. By making your point concisely you'll stand the greatest possible chance of avoiding the undignified fate of being deleted.

Online writing style

As far as writing style is concerned, here, more than with any other medium, it's very, very helpful to write as people speak.

In addition, it will make your email clearer and more concise if you leave out all but essential adjectives and adverbs. Keep your sentences short and only ever include one main idea or thought per sentence. Paragraphs shouldn't consist of more than six sentences max – fewer if possible. And if you need to list more than a couple of items, use bullet points.

Email signatures

If you write emails for business, make good use of the signature facility that goes after your name.

It's surprising just how many people fail to use that facility properly – yet it's an excellent opportunity for you to put across a few words of promotion. Because the email signature appears at the end, your recipients are not likely to be irritated by it. In fact, provided that it contains useful contact information it will be seen as a helpful addition to your message.

Email subject lines

Just as in bricks-and-mortar life, there are no guarantees with email. These days, people have become so hardened to spam that offers them anything from an improved sex life to the chance to babysit an African fortune, you can't blame them for being hesitant – especially if they don't know you well.

Writing effective subject lines has become more difficult now that many people have installed spam filters with teeth like a Rottweiler's. So efficient are those filters at chopping out anything they don't like that now many genuine, personal messages can't get through. To call the whole subject line issue an uphill struggle is an understatement.

Sprinting past the spam filters

First of all you need to know what words not to use, to give your message a fighting chance of getting past the Rottweilers. Words like "email", "marketing", "free", "save", "money", "sex" and (funnily enough) the words "spam" and "you", all tend to get the chop and the rest of the message with it. So do "$$$" and "£££" signs, exclamation marks and sometimes subject lines written all in capital letters.

The latest information on spam filters can be found via some of the US marketing websites like *Clickz.com* and as the picture changes almost from week to week, it's worth keeping up with it. However, as a rough guide, forget any word that appears commonly on the spam subject lines you receive – assuming you don't have a spam filter – and all words that smack of hardsell "stack 'em high, sell 'em cheap" advertising.

Is it really a lost cause?

So having depressed both you and myself totally about subject lines, what can I salvage from all that and use to help you?

Obviously a great deal depends on why you're emailing the person concerned, and if it's a personal email or to a colleague or client you know well, you can write pretty much what you like within reason. Just a quick word here, though – always write *something* rather than leave a blank "message from the internet", even if it's to a friend. It makes it more interesting and helps them prioritize it.

Subject lines for business

As we're discussing business email, though, here are some ideas to make your subject lines more compelling and openable.

Short subject lines are a good idea, a) because they're easy to absorb and b) because on some email clients, only the first few words of a subject line can be read anyway. If you can keep the count to about five words your line will be noticeable in among all the other, longer lines.

Many experts say that your subject line needs as much work on it as the rest of the email and should be a distillation of the gist of your message. I think that might be overdoing it a little, but certainly the advice is useful – try to capture the essence of your message in the most positive way you can.

The other key point is to try to make your subject line sound as natural as possible – anything that looks contrived or glitzy will suggest spam.

Put them on a promise

Always remember that even if you're emailing your granny, a subject line that carries a hint of something in it for her will get her clicking on it a lot faster than a line that says "My cat died". A promise of good things to come is a good attention getter/keeper, provided it's true and of course, natural-sounding.

Questions – intelligent questions, not "would you like to make a fortune?" – work well too, but consequently they've been overused and may now get the Rottweilers' ears pricked. However you can always ask a question without using the ???.

To name or not to name

There is debate over using someone's name in the subject line. Some experts say it's a good idea if you know the name and others say it's only the spammers who do it (and so often get it wrong).

My feeling is, avoid using a name unless there's a very good reason for it and especially if it's to someone who doesn't know you. It may be OK in the US and the Antipodes where people tend to be more open-minded, but in Europe people feel there's something creepy about a total stranger addressing you by name.

Contrarily, using your own name can be helpful especially for regular email communications.

Websites

Thousands of experts far more expert than me have written far more expert pieces on how to write for websites. However, having been around the block a few times myself, I have some views on writing for websites and blogs that you might find helpful.

Web text

One of the problems with websites is that often they have a dozen different jobs to do, most or all of which demand different styles of writing – e.g. sharp sales copy, corporate information, technical guidance, editorial/journalistic, etc – all within the same site.

I think you need to ensure your site is very, very easy to navigate and that the home and landing page or pages in particular direct visitors efficiently to where they want to go. Write your introductory text in as simple and direct a way as you can, choosing the right words to help visitors find what they want quickly and easily. Then ensure that the more specific content is simple, direct and concisely written too, within its own particular style.

Online copy

Before we go on, it may be helpful to define a term or two. As you probably know, in online circles you'll hear the words "copy" and "content". Normally "copy" is the same as in the offline world, i.e. advertising copy. Online ad copy is a specialized area in itself and here are a couple of good sites where you'll find a lot of helpful hints on how to do it well:

http://www.marketingprofs.com
http://www.nickusborne.com

Online content

"Content" is a term I loathe because it has its roots in the days when the words were something a web designer was obliged to find a dusty little corner for on his/her otherwise visually wonderful website. Currently it's used to describe pretty well all pieces of online communication – articles, videos, webinars, white papers, technical data, FAQs, press releases, eBooks, you name it. To avoid this somewhat unfair discrimination where writing is concerned, however, I think it's better to talk about *web text* which covers it all.

A PC/laptop/mobile device or any other form of screen is literally "in yer face", as the Brits say. Especially if you've remembered to switch on your audio speakers, you're very close to the medium emotionally as well as physically.

I think that's another reason why boring, pompous corporate-speak and other forms of bad writing that may escape our loathing offline, jump out and throttle us when we read them from a web-based location. Radio writers always say you haven't got an audience of thousands, you've got thousands of audiences of one. Websites, and especially blogs, are like radio in that way.

Borrow this idea when you're writing web text. Write not to your marketplace or audience, but to one member of it. If you feel uncomfortable writing, sit down with an audio recorder and speak, imagining that you're having a chat with that person over a cup of coffee.

Say your stuff, transcribe it, tidy it up, remove any unnecessary words and phrases and there you are with first draft web text. It may sound simplistic, but it works.

Search engines

I can already hear the screams of indignant protest from my more technically minded readers, but I'll take a chance and say this: search engines are the "Yellow Pages" of the online world. And just as companies in the past would call themselves "AAA Plumbing" or "Aardvark Cabs" to get listed at the beginning of a relevant section, there are ways of writing your website text to improve your ranking on search engines. (NB: changing your company name to Aardvark doesn't work online!)

As you know, SEO (Search Engine Optimization) and search engine marketing are entire industries in their own right. Essentially (and I can hear the SEO experts screaming at me already) it's about deciding which words people would key into the search box when looking for a product or service like yours, and then ensuring that there are as many matches to that as possible within your web text. That, of course, is the tip of the iceberg and the whole process is very much more complex. I would be foolish even to try explaining it here, so do yourself a huge favor and check out the site and advice of my good friend *Nikki Pilkington*, who is one of the leading SEO and internet marketing experts in Europe. *http://nikkipilkington.com*

She explains everything in language even idiots like me can understand.

International audience

You may know exactly where to find your primary "bricks-and-mortar" marketplace or audience, but once you go online they could be anywhere in the world – and not just the online time-wasters (AKA surfers) either. Big business could loom for most of us in any far-flung location.

The consequence for your writing? You need to leave out figurative language, puns, plays on words, and any other quirk that's peculiar to your nationality/region of English, and even just to English, period. If you use humor, make sure it's making the joke about a situation, not about people.

You also need to make as many efforts as are reasonable to ensure you don't write anything that could offend people wherever they are in the world. Obviously you can't be expected to know the finer courtesies of absolutely every culture. However, whether humor is an issue or not, avoid writing anything potentially controversial about sex, race, gender, nationality, religion, politics and any other sensitive area.

Non-linear environment

Websites can't have a beginning, a middle and an end like brochures or other forms of print do. Well, you can have a beginning with a website because usually you control your visitors' landing page, but then they're free to go wherever they like. Don't look upon this as a disadvantage, though, because it liberates you as much as it does your visitors.

With a brochure or catalogue you really need to second-guess your readers and order your content accordingly. Of course readers are free to read from the back to the front, but not everyone does.

Websites require a much more informal order of information. You need to bear that in mind when you're writing the text, and make each section capable of standing alone. Don't assume someone will have read the home page or the introductory paragraphs, because there's a good chance they haven't. Keep that in mind for every web page you write (without being too repetitive, of course) and you can't go far wrong.

Cheap space

Although your website should be written in a way that's crisp and to the point, this does not mean that you have to restrict the range and variety of information. On the contrary. One of the beauties of a website is that it can offer a great deal of information to visitors who want to read it all. And unlike with a glossy brochure, it doesn't cost much to include really quite substantial amounts of extra text.

Also unlike a brochure, where everything is visible on the printed pages, technical or other detailed information on a website stays neatly tucked out of sight until a visitor clicks on it. In fact, depending on the nature of your business, including a lot of detail and relevant in-depth information as an option for visitors to read will make your site "stickier", as they say. Provided the quality of information is good, your site will become a respected reference resource within your marketplace.

Blogs and blogging

What's different about blogging? What does it really mean?

Sarah Arrow, blogger extraordinaire and my partner in crime on HowToWriteBetter, is far better qualified to answer these questions than I am. Here's what she wrote in a recent post on HTWB…

"With a book, a magazine, comic or report, if the writing doesn't grab you, you move to the next section or save it until you are in the right mood. You can read your book/magazine/newspaper pretty much anywhere… even the bath. You can't do that with a blog even if you read it on the Kindle or iPad.

To me that is a key difference between writing and blogging; the setting where the words are going to be read.

Do you write differently online than you do offline?

Of course you do. Offline, you don't care about seeing keywords are in the text, or the keyword density, or that your title is clickable (although you may worry about it being readable.)

If your writing is good it sells more articles or converts to more sales (or whatever your call to action is). If your blogging is good it will do the same. But if your blogging is not so good, no matter how you promote it you just won't get read.

Again another difference; a writer walks away and cashes their cheque, a blogger has to promote and entice their audience to interact as well as read the article."

Why is blogging different from article writing?

Recently I put up a post on Facebook suggesting that maybe blogging and journalism are approaching something of a head-to-head online, considering the way that all our news and features media seem to be merging. The reactions I got were quite stark.

One US TV journalist said the key differences between the two are the fact that journalists have deadlines and editors to contend with – major issues bloggers don't share, and that's true, for sure. Someone else sent me a private message saying the two disciplines had nothing whatsoever to do with each other and I should be ashamed of myself for even suggesting there might be a conflict here.

When you strip the whole blogging story down to its underwear, you can see where the journos are coming from in their somewhat dismissive attitude towards bloggers. Blogging started out as an online platform for "journaling", which is light years away from journalism.

Journaling: not the same as keeping a diary, but not reporting either

I won't refer you to any onward links here, although there are several on Google, but essentially the difference between keeping a diary and journaling is this: a diary is purely a record of your events – a journal is a record of your events along with your comments and views about those events.

This is where blogging started and, as we all know, it has evolved dramatically, which is where the dividing line between it and journalism begins to dissolve slightly. Many blogs today – deliberately or accidentally – cross over the invisible line into what perhaps we should call "alternative online journalism". But should bloggers begin to think of themselves as journalists? Hmmm...

How do the journalists feel?

When you ask a journalist how they regard bloggers, their answers have a tendency to be negative. However you can't be surprised to find that traditional, professional journalism appears to be threatened not just by bloggers, but by the entire freedom of the internet which gallops over many disciplines like young horses having just broken out of a field.

Obviously, when you consider news reporting there's

no contest. But it's in the area of features, and particularly journalistic opinion pieces, where the potential conflict may lie. Journalists have spent years studying and serving apprenticeships so they can report and comment in a professional way about the topics they cover. But in recent years, along comes the internet and opens up a huge new forum in which anybody can report on events and express opinions... unfettered by editorial policy, deadlines, or – let's face it – ethical considerations.

Could journaling and journalism share a future?

This is something that worries me, and I'm sure worries many journalists. Although I have spent many years writing in the utterly commercial sector, I was trained originally as a journalist (served my apprenticeship on a UK local newspaper). And when I write posts like this, I try as far as I can to be fair and represent – or at least point out – all points of view.

But this is blogging. Where could it lead us? Should it attempt to swamp good old-fashioned traditional journalism? Or should we all work towards maintaining a respectful division between the two?

You might like to take a look at *"A Blogger's Code of Ethics"* from *CyberJournalist.net* (a very useful and up-to-date resource dealing with just these issues.) It attempts to, a) suggest how bloggers should approach their responsibility to their readers, and b) differentiate themselves from professional journalists.

And what about personal blogs?

Personal blogs don't have to connect with your business, of course. But as we move increasingly towards an ultra-personal environment for business communication, there is a correspondingly growing interest in what we have to say about ourselves at a personal level. Who we are as individuals inevitably influences what we do for the day job."

From one of my recent posts on HTWB...

"Many people view their blogs almost as online journals – in fact that's how the whole blogging concept started. In this case you use it to record what's going on in your life, key events and your thoughts about them, and anything else that takes your fancy.

However you could be running a personal blog alongside a business or special interest blog. In this case, as there will be linking between them, your personal content needs to be mindful about what you say in the other one or ones."

First person, second person, third person?

The internet is informal, and blogging is an even more informal manifestation of that. So to blog in the third person – especially when it is a personal blog – would seem ridiculous. Whatever you write is going to be seen as coming from you, the person (not the brand) and perhaps your partner and family.

Using the second person (i.e. "we") when you're describing the fun you and the kids had at the safari park is perfectly OK. However you must avoid anything that smells of the "royal we" when what you really mean is "I". Once again, informality is key on the internet and anything even vaguely pompous or patronizing sticks out like the proverbial sore thumb.

What's in it for them?

Although a personal blog necessarily is going to be more "me" focused than, say, marketing or promotional text, you still don't want to ram too much of "me" down your readers' throats. (Remember the old joke about the conceited actor who bored his date to tears talking about himself for hours, then finally turned to her and said, "Well, that's enough about me. Now, what do *you* think about me?")

My interpretation of a good personal blog is the way "I" (i.e. author) share my experiences, thoughts and conclusions in an entertaining and meaningful way with "you", the reader, so that "you" the reader get as much out of what I write as "I" do. That's not a commercial statement, or indeed a commercially adequate proposal – but with human nature being as selfish as it is, it's a reality.

So once again, when writing we must keep one eye on the old advertising adage of always ensuring you focus on "what's in it for them", your readers. You can't expect many return visits or onward sharing of your posts if readers find them boring, self-congratulatory, narrow-minded, or bigoted in any way.

Themes

Strictly speaking, your personal blog does not have to have a particular theme or slant, but unless you're a famous actor, pop star or reality TV personality, the harsh truth is people will not be interested in a blog that's just about you and your day-to-day life.

Your personal blog's theme doesn't need to be anything exotic; it just needs to help create a focus for what you have to say. This could be your favourite hobby... your location/environment... your family and parenting... your way of life... your faith and what that entails... etc. Don't restrict yourself unnecessarily, but at the same time don't let your blog drift without some sort of direction.

A perfect essay?

Blog posts do not have to be perfectly crafted pieces of prose – in fact that's the beauty of blogging; total de-restriction on earlier modes of communication and the freedom to do and say what you like without someone criticizing you for it.

Well, that's the theory, anyway. Whether we cyber-hippies like it or not, however, the bottom line is that badly crafted and badly written blog posts say about as much for you as if you to wear a dirty old shirt and jeans to a formal gala event. If you want credibility and respect, you have to write reasonably well and construct your blog posts properly.

What's "properly"? Well, again, we're not talking university level language here, but on the other hand your grammar, syntax, punctuation and spelling need to be pretty much OK if you're to retain the respect of your readers. Your posts need to stay on topic without wandering off into the wild blue yonder and ideally need to have a beginning, a middle and an end.

Beware the dangers of BS blogging…

Another post from HTWB where I highlight what can go horribly wrong with blogging…

"We've seen it all in various media – beautifully crafted phrases and sentences that seem like first class writing, but when you analyse what they actually convey, the answer is three-fifths of ****-all.

And in our current feeding frenzy of frequent blogging on anything from international diplomacy to stick-insect rearing, we've provided ourselves with the perfect breeding ground for much more meaningless, well-written drivel."

Because the pressure is on us bloggers – especially business bloggers – to keep adding new content at breakneck speed to feed the Googlybots and other slavering cybermonsters, so we keep ourselves fresh and perky for SEO, there comes a time when we might be tempted to write about not very much... and disguise it by crafting it in perfect, elaborate English.

But that's not good blogging; that's "good" b*llsh*t

I have a lot of time for organisations like the UK's *http://PlainEnglishCampaign.co.uk* which has been battling for years to stop organisations – particularly government and other public bodies – from issuing information in technically perfect English that not only says nothing, but is also utter garbage.

If you have a couple of minutes to spare and want a good laugh, have a look at their *gobbledygook generator page http://www.plainenglish.co.uk/examples/gobbledygook-generator.html on* their site. You just click and you get some instant b*llsh*t that sounds truly clever and worthy. A couple of – well, three – examples when I clicked just now...

> *"It's time that we became uber-efficient with our responsive strategic time-phases."*

> *"We need a more contemporary reimagining of our ambient third-generation options."*

> *"I can make a window to discuss your balanced transitional options."*

But enough with the hilarity. What's especially funny and awful all at the same time is that we see drivel like that creeping into much of the stuff we read every day – and blogs are often the worst.

What about a badly written blog about something worthwhile and interesting?

Ah, now you have me dithering between the "write properly" fairy and the "don't be picky" demon. If you force me to choose, I would cautiously say, good interesting content is more important.

As *Sarah Arrow* says in *her post* on her own multi-author site, *BirdsOnTheBlog*:

> *"I am sick of people thinking that blogging is the sole domain of writers. There are heaps (130+ million) of blogs out there and you don't have to be the world's most perfect writer to write a blog post. As an average writer I do rather well. I have seen blog posts that are poorly written but express a lot of personality, get a whole heap of comments as well as posts that are beautifully written, perfect grammar and don't even get a tweet let alone a comment."*

So what's the bottom line?

Simple: find something interesting to write about, then write it in your blog. If you can't think of anything good to write about, don't write drivel and glam it up with fancy words or elegant turns of phrase.

You might be able to generate something like that, stuff it full of keywords and links and please the cybermonsters, but your readers – some of whom may be customers or clients, too – will think you're a jerk. I still believe that quality content wins every time and it would take wild horses to drag me out of that conviction.

But to sum it all up...

Sarah: ...when people write from their hearts they get a better response which is why a controversial post will do better than a bland toe the line post. The controversial blogger is saying "agree with me or disagree with me" and a discussion starts.

Suze: I think you've identified what differentiates blogging from other forms of writing – blogging is writing from the heart. That's as opposed to reporting, discussing, commentating, etc which are all more traditional journalistic techniques.

Where this gets really interesting is in corporate blogging circumstances. Blogging from the heart of a major brand is a lot harder than from your own heart. All the same, that's what readers want these days – major brands can't get away with the corporate b*llsh*t any more and it's a good thing, too.

Sarah Arrow has published an excellent book about blogging which tells you everything you need to know about setting up your blog in the first place, how to create the image, look and content you want, and how to promote it.

For more information, go to
http://www.saraharrow.co.uk

Mobile communications

This is an area of increasing importance today and is a very, very long way from those geeky SMS/text messages of the "CU 18er" variety we've been used to for some years.

Because you can now surf the internet using your mobile device, business communicators are having to take another look – and rather a long, considered look – at how their websites and blogs translate on to what we old goats describe as gizmos smaller than cigarette packs on which we're expected to read the entire content of the universe.

Word on the street is, many businesses are adopting an attitude of "let's see if our main website works for mobile", rather than rethinking their content and messages for a medium that is very different from the full-blown www.

Being an utter Luddite, I don't have one of these fancy phones that allow you to surf the net – yet – so the other day I asked a friend to put up HowToWriteBetter.net on his touch phone to see how it looked in miniature.

Well, of course, I needed the reading glasses to see anything at all even though as he stroked the screen bigger and bigger images came up. And as HTWB.net is pretty straightforward with few frills, I wasn't too disappointed in the result.

But what happens with sites – even blogsites – that are much more complex than mine?

I shudder to think. I know younger folks have good eyesight and these touchy-feely devices are able to magnify text to an extent where even I can read it without glasses.

However, an alarmingly large number of websites and even blogs translate very poorly to mobile. And although it's not really within my remit to comment on it, it's worth flagging up and thinking about how your own site or blog works on the weenie-screens.

And writing for mobile?

Well, until these mobile devices manage to implant a device in people's brains which allow unlimited communication, you guessed it...

Brief, short, sharp and direct is what's needed, especially when you're squinting at such a small screen.

As for audio and video on mobile? Interesting... and especially with audio, could offer some exciting possibilities that could compensate for mobiles' – so far – visual limitations.

Writing for PR

Print newsletters

PRINT NEWSLETTERS HAVE A SAD habit of falling prey to the same self-indulgent and boring content as the misguided, subjective, self-congratulatory press releases so many organisations issue. Only this time, it's worse. It's not just a few paragraphs of self-indulgent drivel, it's two, four or even eight pages of stuff that's of tremendous interest to the writers and instigators, but usually of no interest to the readers.

Of course, if the newsletter is directed only to staff or another purely internal group, the fact that there is a certain degree of family indulgence will help.

Where you do have to pull yourselves up by the bootlaces is with newsletters that go outside the organization – particularly customer newsletters. Here you need to place yourself firmly in the shoes of the audience and ensure that your content is of interest to them.

Valuable information for readers

Newsletters are of much greater value to the reader if they contain information that is of genuine, generic use to them – information that helps them do their jobs better, or in some other way improves their daily life.

Very few people these days are stupid enough to be fooled by the thinly disguised advertising blurb masquerading as "useful" editorial. Yet all too often I see companies spending quite large sums of money on customer newsletters that really do put the "junk" into junk mail.

All it takes to turn a boring, totally subjective newsletter into a useful, interesting one is a little time and imagination, not big bucks.

- **A car dealership**'s quarterly newsletter can not only announce the latest new model launches and new staff appointments, but also include a seasonal maintenance checklist: how to drive safely in winter conditions; ideas on how to keep the kids entertained on long car trips; security and anti-theft tips; dates of future roadworks/construction that may cause congestion, etc.

- **An accountancy firm** can send out information on how new legislation affects local or regional businesses, how new tax laws should be interpreted, tips and advice on how to fill out personal tax returns, tips for small businesses and self-employed people on how to record their expenses more efficiently, etc.

- **An investment company** can send out information to business customers that updates them on the latest corporate issues and how those apply to individual companies, and also include advice on personal investments, pension plans, even advice for readers' families, e.g. saving for college/university loans and the best savings plans to set up for children, trust funds, etc.

All of the information I've described above would not cost much to procure – probably just a matter of a few phone calls, a couple of hours surfing the net, and a day or two of someone's time putting it all together. Obviously you need to be careful not to use other organizations' copyright material without permission, but in my experience, most organizations will cheerfully grant you permission provided that you credit them appropriately.

What a difference this type of content makes to an organization's external newsletter! You instantly gain the respect of your readers, because you're giving them something tangible without asking them for anything in return. And this can only reflect in one way on your business relationship with them.

Online newsletters

In much the same way as the paper-based newsletter, the online version will be taken much more seriously by its readers if, in addition to the necessary reminders about your products and services, you also include some genuinely useful and interesting information. However the online version, in keeping with most other online descendants of offline media, must be much shorter and far more condensed.

Traffic to your website or blog

One of the primary uses of e-newsletters is to "drive traffic to the website/blog". Now, in itself this is relatively harmless and provided that everything is done right, it usually works. And then once you've got visitors hooked into all your superb content on the website or blog, you have a captive audience to whom you can sell your own stuff if it's a company-only site, or your advertisers' stuff if it's a more open-ended one. Or at least that's the theory.

However, as you would expect, some organizations get this hideously wrong and, in my view, the most vivid example of it is the online newsletter that comprises little more than a sentence or two about something followed by a clickable link. Nothing, but nothing, is more irritating to someone like me than an enticing e-newsletter with grabby headlines plus a few words leading into the topic and then... nothing. If I can be bothered to click through to the site to read more, chances are I won't go back to the newsletter afterwards.

Make sure it contains value

If you're in a position to choose how an online newsletter is put together and you want to get the best possible results from it, please, please remember to put enough into it so there's something "in it for them"'.

Of course, if you have a website you'll want to drive traffic to it. But create a realistic balance – don't be so naïve as to think you can force people to click on to your website by dangling a carrot just out of their reach. As I suggested, if they're anything like me they'll feel resentful and antagonized by it and will resolve never to visit your site even if dragged there by wild horses.

My own personal preference is the standalone variety of online newsletter that makes clicking through to the website merely an optional extra. But I know that in a business context this is not as commercially attractive. So probably the next best thing is online newsletters that supply the audience with a summary or shortened version of the content so they get the key points and refer them to the website for further details.

That's an acceptable balance that will encourage people to click through to the site if they have a genuine interest plus the time to spare, and if they haven't time at least they'll remember you and your summaries fondly and be more inclined to click through to the site next time.

Press releases: offline

Time after time after time I'm called into companies and asked to comment on why the PR coverage they get in the media is so poor. 99 times out of a 100 it's because they've issued press releases that are only of interest to themselves and their bosses.

And yet when I point this out to them they can't

understand it. "But our development team worked 14 hours a day for three years to win that contract!" they shout indignantly. "And the CEO had to cut short his vacation in Turks & Caicos just so he could sign the documents by the deadline!" Sorry folks, but media audiences don't care.

Forget self-congratulation

If you want to get coverage in the media then you must forget all elements of self-congratulation. The information you send out has to have something "in it for them" (the audience) – something new, interesting and relevant. It doesn't have to be earth-shattering, just worth reading.

And you don't simply have the audience to consider in this case. Because unlike the forms of communication you control, with media coverage the decision of whether or not to transmit your message rests with someone else – usually the editor.

If you supply them with material they can see is relevant to their readers and preferably is usable with the minimum of editing, they will warm to it a lot faster than something that may hold a grain of interest but will take someone a whole evening to rewrite and several phone calls or e-mails to check for accuracy.

Write in the style of the publication

Try to match the style and writing approach of the publication. If you're sending a release out to several publications that circulate among the same readership, then one release should be relevant to all.

But if you're aiming at different press groups – say the trade journals/websites and the business pages of the regional sites and papers – you need to rework the approach of your press release according to the various audiences involved.

You'll often find that the basic core of a press release can remain pretty well the same across all media groups, because it consists (or should consist) of the pure facts – the old journalist's formula of who, what, how, where, when and why.

What changes is the angle, and particularly the lead-in. That means the headline, which should be short and attention-grabbing, and then the first two or three sentences that support the headline and set up the whole story.

Know the readership

A good way to nail down the appropriate style and approach is to read and become familiar with the publication/website/etc you're aiming at. By far the best guidance you'll get, though, comes from studying the audience – the people who read the publications.

What in your story is going to interest them? Readers of a trade journal or online site/blog/etc will be interested in what's new and different about your new product and how it could improve the way they do business.

Readers of local or regional business sites and publications will be interested more in how your new product's manufacturing and distribution, say, will impact on the local business community and economy.

Local general newspapers and other media will be interested in the human side, i.e. how many new jobs the factory producing the new product will create.

Use "quotes" creatively

And one last tip on how to get the best from press releases – use "quotes" from the key people involved in the story.

Whatever you do, don't use those awful, meaningless, corporate-babble quotes you so often see in company press releases... "We are delighted to be able to announce the new contract at this moment in time and we have every confidence that our latest investment will be of significant benefit to our..." you know the type of thing. These are usually the first elements that get chopped out by the editor.

Instead, generate (and yes, it's OK to write quotes as long as the "quoters" see them first and approve them) fact-rich quotes that tell important parts of the story. The publication's staff will be far less likely to edit those out.

Press releases: online

There are two different issues here and let's look at them in turn.

- Online media
- Email press releases

Often the two go together, but they don't always – for example, it's quite common to email press releases to print publications. Anyway, let's look at online media first.

Online media

Nearly all the theory pertaining to offline PR is relevant to the online equivalent – especially in terms of what content is of interest to publishers and what isn't.

Online publishing of relevance to organizations usually falls into one of two pretty obvious groups:

1. Websites, portals etc that are totally independent and uniquely on the web, and
2. Those which are the online alter egos of offline publications

In either group if you want the publications to take your releases or submissions seriously, it's very important that you follow the format and structure of articles that appear on the websites concerned. Whatever you do, don't make the mistake of submitting a general press release to these organizations, even though you do it by e-mail.

Check first the length of the "teaser paragraph" or abstract that appears on the home or section page, and check how they lay out the full articles. Then submit material that fits perfectly, both in style and in word counts. You will be saving them the trouble of reworking your piece, which makes it attractive in the first place; and, because it fits so perfectly, you will discourage them from changing anything, which is also a huge advantage for you. Even if they do change what you've written, they'll be flattered that you took the trouble to design your release around their online publication, which in itself can put you in a favorable light.

The other point I would make about online press work is, don't assume that just because you submit a release to the offline publication (and even if they run it) it will be forwarded automatically to the publication's website.

Treat offline and online versions as entirely separate entities. Find out who the movers and shakers are on each, and often you'll see that the online version is run by an entirely different group of people.

Email press releases

Many people feel that email press releases should be shorter than their hardcopy equivalents. But as I believe that hardcopy releases should be pretty short and snappy too, I don't personally feel there is a lot of difference.

Essentially, to do well with these you need to combine the "rules" of writing good press releases with the "rules" of good online writing.

Use the subject line as a crystallization of your story's "hook" – preferably in fewer than five words, so editors and journalists will get the message even if their email system cuts long subject lines down.

Start the body of the email text with one line that says "news from XXXX" and then go straight into your attention grabbing headline, which may well be a slightly longer version of the subject line.

Then, ensure that your first, short paragraph sums up the main gist of the story, with the who, what, why, when, where, and how developed further in a few short, snappy supporting paragraphs.

Don't add in more than the most essential detail and background. At the end, refer readers to "Notes For Editors" for background information.

If your website isn't up to scratch then it is just about OK to append a short section of "Notes to Editors" after the main body of the press release.

Make your website or blog press-friendly

Ideally you should have a "press room" on the site, but it's not essential if you're just starting out or don't do much PR. However it's categorized, you need to supply all the background information about your company and its senior people, activities, locations, etc.

If you have a press room you can also include downloadable photographs and other relevant stuff like the white papers, e-books, research reports, etc, that you've done.

And finally, if you have a press room – or even if you don't – make sure your website is always, always up to date. There's nothing that looks more amateurish to a journalist than a long list of press releases that were issued three years ago. Yet having taken a look at several company website press rooms in the last few weeks, I know that happens all too frequently.

No attachments

Journalists and editors (and their bosses) are rightly terrified of viruses and will not open attachments unless they know you better than their own mothers. Never, ever use an attachment for PR purposes unless you have spoken with the journalist previously and arranged it.

Also, you should bear in mind that journalists working for smaller publications, and also some freelance journalists, may not appreciate having to download huge files of complex pictures and graphics unless they specifically ask for it. For this reason, in your email press releases you should mention what material is available and ask them to reply to your message stating what they want you to send.

Finally, email press releases should always provide your name, company name, postal address and phone numbers to help establish who you are and give journalists the chance to phone you for more information – something many "journos" prefer.

Writing articles

Writing articles on your topic (or your business's topic) is usually a useful PR opportunity, a) because it publicizes you /your organization and b) because it can raise your profile as an expert on the topic concerned.

Online, this is sometimes called "article marketing", but be warned: many such "articles" are gibberish – literally, nonsensical automated rewrites of one piece generated to provide "original" articles full of links and keywords to attract the search engines. This is not the sort of article writing I recommend!

Articles (proper ones!) are different from press releases because they're usually longer and in "feature" style, i.e. not using the hard-nosed news approach of most press releases. Articles in this context are usually more relaxed and more detailed, taking a more in-depth look at the subject matter.

Please note that when I refer to a "publication", I mean either offline or online. So what are they key issues to bear in mind?

1. Articles are not advertising

… even if you've paid for an ad space in a publication and the "free editorial" is part of the package. Sure, with a package like that the publication will accept whatever you want to say in the editorial (and I won't go into what my personal opinion on that here!) But if you want people to read beyond the first sentence, your article needs to be an article, not advertising or brochure copy written in an editorial style.

2. Articles are about information

… because that's why people read magazines, business publications, etc. OK, there may be a certain entertainment element but primarily you read the sort publications we're talking about here to increase your knowledge. If you want to be asked to contribute to a publication again, you must write responsibly. Only use your opinions for an article if you've earned the right to express them. Always check facts and figures, because if you get them wrong it reflects badly not only on you but also on the publication.

3. Readers are only interested in themselves

… and that means everything you put in your article must be, as far as possible, something that would interest them, not you or your boss. To find out what interests readers you need to research who they are and what makes them tick.

4. *Keeping readers' interest means giving them value*

… which means you either have to tell something interesting that they don't already know, tell them how to do something better, or give advice on an issue which you know (from your research) is likely to be of concern to them, etc.

5. *If you can't give advice, tell a story*

… because people like real "slice of life" anecdotes as long as they're relevant. Ditto with case histories, provided that you keep them brief and succinct. If your service or product involves solving people's problems, don't just say so – that's a) advertising and b) boring. Use a real example of how it has solved people's problems. Use quotes from the people concerned. Bring your article to life.

6. *Length is important*

… because editors are busy people and if they don't have to cut or pad out your contribution they'll love you for it. Find out how many words they want from you and ensure you submit that many (within 20 words or so). You don't want others tinkering with your words, do you? And knowing ahead of time how many words to write helps give you a feel for how much detail you need to include before you start writing. Submitting an article that's the correct length helps to make you look professional, and you're more likely to get asked to contribute again.

Now, let's look at some crafting pointers.

Crafting pointer #1: Devise a strong theme and stick to it

Assuming that you haven't been told what to write about by the publication's editor, decide this on the basis of what you believe will interest readers most and then stick to it firmly. Help yourself to stick to the point by writing out a content skeleton in bullet point form. Then start adding "flesh to the bones" as notes. Only start writing the article when you've defined and organized your content to your satisfaction.

Crafting pointer #2: Get your "tone of voice" right"

Whatever you do, don't fall into the trap of assuming a tone of voice which you think is appropriate for your organization's image, unless it's identical to the right one for the audience. Read as many back issues of the publication concerned as you can get hold of, so you get the feel for their own editorial. Then copy that.

Crafting pointer #3: Avoid unfriendly jargon

Particularly in technical publications, a certain amount of jargon is OK because the readership is likely to be familiar with it. However be sure you check this very carefully and don't allow any suspect jargon to creep into what you write. Also, don't take a chance on people not understanding acronyms, abbreviations, etc. If in doubt, spell it out.

Crafting pointer #4: Devise a snappy headline

Although the publication's editor may well change it, making the headline good will help ensure that the final version remains as close to your original as possible. Once again, look at back numbers of the publication for an indication of style and approach. Generally it's best to keep it simple, direct; try to make it imply a benefit to the reader. Only attempt a "clever" headline (pun, play on catchphrase, etc) if you know you're really good at it – and that the pun is consistent with the general flow of the piece. A pun purely for its own sake isn't worthwhile.

Crafting pointer #5: Create a sharp summary/intro paragraph

This is something that's more of an issue in online press releases, but I think it's a useful device for any article. In two or three sentences, summarize the key message of your article and then use that as an introductory paragraph. The editor may not leave it there, but if – as is often the case – s/he uses a trailer for your article on the front page or on the publication's website, etc, that's what they'll use or base it on, anyway. Extra-tip: write this para after you've written the article. Don't try to start with it as you'll find yourself going into too much detail.

Crafting pointer #6: Stick to a structure with "how to"

In a "how to" article your structure is fairly easy to define. First you set up the topic, then go through your tips on how to do it pretty much in chronological order, and finish off with a short summary or conclusion. Don't use any detail that isn't strictly relevant to what your reader needs. However at the same time, be careful you don't wrongly assume prior knowledge on the part of the reader. Be sure you know how much they know.

Crafting pointer #7: Use quotes to help tell a story

Although any story you tell in a business article is going to be true, it helps to take some tips from fiction writers and use a bit of drama to bring the story alive. Instead of starting predictably with the background of the case history and how you came to meet the customer, etc, start with a blazing quote from the customer him/herself – "I was up to my knees in water and could see my entire stock being destroyed," said Jerry Kann, Production Manager of XYZ Clothing Manufacturers. "When you and your pumping crew turned up so quickly I could have kissed you all..." Don't be afraid to use quotes. As long as they're real and don't contain pompous corporate-speak, they're very powerful.

Crafting pointer #8: Edit hard but sensibly

To be honest, not many of us have the time to hone our writing by producing umpteen drafts and in any case I believe you can over-edit your work, making it too dry and unspontaneous. However hard editing is necessary, especially if your first draft is over length. If you need to cut out more than, say, 20%, don't try to shorten everything. If you do, you're bound to strangle some of your good points. Instead ask yourself if all your content is really necessary, and if some points are not strictly required, then dump them. If the article is seriously over length and you can't justify giving it a good haircut, contact the editor and ask if they can run it over two issues in two parts.

Online articles

If you're asked to submit an article to a website, obviously you will discuss the content, tone, length etc with the people concerned before you start. Sometimes, though, you'll be given a free rein.

If this is the case, choose your subject matter very carefully. Even if the site owners tell you to write about anything you want, make sure you understand their typical audience and choose a topic that will be of genuine news or feature value to them. OK, by all means work in a few mentions of your product or service but remember this: readers aren't stupid. If your article looks like a thinly disguised advertisement your credibility will be down the toilet. It's a simple as that.

If you have a free rein over length, don't go much beyond 800-1,000 words. One of the websites I write for, *http://www.marketingprofs.com*, has found that this is the optimum length to retain people's attention and concentration, because more often than not they will read the article online (rather than print it out and read it off paper later.)

Keep to simple structure and style

Structure-wise, use shorter sentences and shorter paragraphs than you do for print articles. Every few paragraphs, break the text up with a snappy, relevant cross-heading.

Style-wise, keep your language simple and uncluttered. Avoid unnecessarily long words and phrases. Be direct and write to the reader. If you find this hard to grasp, imagine you're writing a letter to one typical member of the website's audience. Have a picture of that person in your mind. Visualize what s/he will find interesting and what will begin to bore him/her. I know that sounds weird and psychobabblesque, but it works to keep you reader-focused.

Finally – and I say this deliberately, because it's far easier to do it last than first – write a trailer paragraph (an abstract) about your article. You should include this as an emboldened introduction to your article, but it should also be able to stand alone so the site can use it as an abstract if they want to. The editor may tinker with this paragraph a bit, but I always prefer to offer them a suggestion of how to introduce my article – rather than let them do it from scratch!

White papers

White papers aren't as fashionable as they once were, but they are still called for from time to time, so it's useful to understand what they do and how to write them.

As you know, white papers differ from articles because they're much longer and because they're supposed to be non-commercial studies, essays, reports and whatever. OK? That means no pluggeroos. Needless to say the reality is somewhat different and commerciality creeps in, sometimes all over the place, which (as it does with articles) discredits your whole piece.

In my view the best way to handle this one is to discuss the issue frankly with the site owners beforehand. Ask them if a realistic and appropriate mention of your product or service is acceptable. Unless they're paying you to write the WP, it's pretty hard for them to say no. Ensure that you stick rigidly to whatever is agreed, and your reputation as an "expert" will be secured.

White papers are more often downloaded as PDF files or similar and then printed out to be read later. In theory, then, you don't have to be quite so careful to structure and style your material to be read from a screen. However people do read white papers on screen, so you need to put the WP together in a way that works across both media.

The host site may well want to set up and format your WP their way and, in that case, all you need do is submit a word-processed document. If you think they may use it as is, though, set it up in an eyeball-friendly font like Times New Roman or Verdana. Bump it up to 14 point and then use bold and one or two colors – no more than that – to cheer it up and emphasize things. This way it will be friendly to read on a screen, but will look OK when printed out, too.

No matter how technical or academic your white paper, never forget the golden online writing rules of keeping it simple, short, crisp and uncluttered. Box off sections of highly technical data, graphs, charts, figures, etc. Avoid using more than essential online links, especially in view of the fact that many of your audience will be reading offline.

ADVERTISING

Overview

I PROBABLY SHOULDN'T GIVE AWAY trade secrets like this, but actually, writing simple ad copy is not rocket science. OK, what you need to write for a major international brand of FMCG product that's virtually identical to 53 others with equally huge advertising budgets, is not easy to get right. But we're talking about the smaller end of the scale here.

Whether it's a recruitment ad for a new member of staff, a property ad to try to sell your home, a classified ad selling your car/bicycle/drum kit or a postcard advertising your product or service, you *can* do it. And do it well.

Here is some information adapted from an article I wrote a while back for the US website, *Marketing Professionals*. Since it went up on the site, the article has been read by more than 11,000 people.

A few of the 40-odd feedback comments (all positive) the article got:

"Clear, clear, clear... the art of putting obvious things in line so that they become a process."

"As a person with no marketing or authoring background, writing copy for a website, this provides me with an essential insight into what I need to say when selling our services. Thanks!"

"Suzan – Absolutely Superb! Key concepts of human communication and comprehension simply stated in bite sized morsels of wisdom... gained from hands-on experience. "

"Best I ever read or heard! Note: If your floor is shaking it's because I am stomping my feet too!"

Sorry, my ego got in the way there. Anyway, my point? It works!

To keep this simple we'll use my old friend, Joe the carpenter, whom I first introduced in *"Powerwriting"*, as our metaphor. I know carpentry doesn't have a lot in common with major business corporations, but the principles of how to approach promotional writing are identical, whatever the subject matter.

So what have we got, with no frills?

Joe the carpenter is really good at making things out of wood

We'll get a lot more done a lot faster if we forget that and instead focus on what we want to achieve.

Joe wants to increase and consolidate his business as a carpenter specializing in woodwork for people's homes in this area.

Now we need to figure out the best way for him to do this. In the advertising world this would be handled by the planners/account team etc, not the copywriter. But we're talking DIY here. So first step is, take a closer look at Joe's target audience. Who are they, and what do they want from carpentry?

Joe the carpenter's potential customers are well-heeled local home owners who are prepared to pay well, but only for high quality work and service they can depend on
What do we deduce from this? Obviously, a low-price story won't impress them. In fact if anything it will put them off Joe.

What is likely to work is a quality story. Also, we notice an element of insecurity here too, which we can use to help establish Joe's reliability. More of that later.

Next consideration is, how are we going to get our message to the marketplace? This can affect what we write.

Joe the carpenter will use quality leaflets, hand-delivered to targeted homes (if he had an appropriate e-mailing list he could use this instead. The following concepts would work across pretty much all relevant media.)

That means his message should be very personal, from me to you. The leaflet (or email) is great because it's highly targeted and there'll be little or no wastage, but we'll have to grab them by the throat from the first line or our message will be in the trashcan.

Now, what have we got to offer that other carpenters haven't? Why should people pick up the phone to call him? Why should they trust him with something as important as the contents of their homes?

- **Joe the carpenter is highly skilled**
- **He has 20 years' experience**
- **He's a local man, born and bred**
- **He's worked for some of the city's most respected residents, including the Mayor – some for many years**
- **He has glowing testimonials from many of his customers who are prepared to say so if a new customer wants to ask them**

That's all excellent stuff, but there's a problem here. Those are features, not benefits. As you know, features are what something or someone – your product – *is* (so what?); and benefits are what it/he/she *does* (for me?

That's more interesting). If you want to write good promotional material, remember this cute little phrase: **features smell, benefits sell.**

To remind you, it's easy to turn a feature into a benefit. Just add a "so" at the end of the feature and fill in the blank. Like this:

Joe the carpenter is highly skilled – so he knows what he is doing and you can rely on that.

He has 20 years' experience – so he won't waste your time or money because he knows what works and what doesn't.

He's a local man, born and bred – so he's not likely to do a moonlight flit having half-completed your work, because people know where to find him.

He's worked for some of the city's most respected residents, including the Mayor – some for many years – so the guy must be doing something right.

He has glowing testimonials from many of his customers who are prepared to say so if a new customer wants to ask them – so we have proof that he's doing something right; these days testimonials legally have to be true.

Now, we need one key benefit for our message to lead with. This is what adfolks call the USP – the Unique Selling Proposition. You get that by asking, what does all this really boil down to? First the feature...

Joe the carpenter is acknowledged as XXXtown's leading quality carpenter for people's homes.

And the resulting benefit – what does this do for you?

Joe the carpenter gives you high-quality carpentry you can really rely on.

So how do we get our message to portray that benefit?

We portray it by implanting a sentiment in our message – one that instantly captures the benefit.

Sentiments don't have to be touchy-feely. They can be based on anything from sex and rock'n'roll to hard-nosed financial or management issues. Whatever the choice, the secret of a message that works is to choose the right sentiment and then use it so the audience immediately grasps the benefits of buying your product or service.

In this case, by adding a sentiment into our message we see a powerful benefit coming through:

Because you really care about the quality of everything in your home, only Joe is good enough to do your carpentry.

That's lumpy, so let's develop a concept that says it in a shorter but sharper way. (Concepts are prettied-up versions of the message, on which you then base your final headlines and copy.)

Only you value the quality of new woodwork in your home as much as Joe the carpenter does.
I like that as a concept, but it might be seen as not hard enough, even for this end of the market. What about a concept that touches on the insecurity issue (mentioned above) as well?

The dependable, handcrafted carpentry service your home deserves... now available from XXXtown's leading expert, Joe the carpenter.

Or this, making even more of that insecurity...

Chances are, most carpenters could do a good job on the woodwork in your home.
If you don't want to leave it to chance, call Joe the carpenter.

All this is the approach I use when writing ad or promotional copy. Other pro writers may take a slightly different approach, but there will be many common denominators because the basic method works.

If I had to pick one single element from this as the most important of all, I'd say remember my cute little phrase: features smell, benefits sell. If everything you write for this purpose is benefits led, you won't ever go far wrong.

Sales letters

Much as we spend most of our lives online, there are still occasions when a printed letter is required, even if all you do with it is to attach it to an email! Here, then, are some tips on how to approach it effectively.

It's important to differentiate here between the really hard-nosed direct mail sales letter and, say, a new business announcement or a covering letter you send out to accompany some marketing or other information to a prospect or customer. The former type is best left to professionals, because it takes a great deal of skill, practice and experience to do it well. The latter kind, though, can be done quite effectively by the DIY sales writer. Here are my thoughts on that.

The one main difference between sales letters and personal letters is the role you play. In a personal letter you write in your own style about what you want to say. In a sales letter your focus is totally on the recipient, and you write in the style that he or she will identify with most readily – regardless of your own personal style. Because of this, your style will vary according to who is going to receive the letter.

Show them you care from line one

Right from the very first line, you need to show your readers that you empathize totally with their needs. The better you do that, the more likely they are to keep reading. To achieve that you need to do your homework, find out what your readers real needs are and focus everything you want to sell them on how it meets those needs and benefits them.

You also need to focus very firmly on "you" and avoid talking more than strictly necessary about "we" and "us", except for where it obviously benefits "you".

Facts, not sales talk

Finally, a good sales letter needs to focus on facts – not selling jargon. Readers aren't stupid. They're not going to be interested in your product or service unless they know precisely what's "in it for them" right from the beginning, and why that's in it for them. The only credible way to answer the "why" part is to give truthful, straight facts. The selling skill isn't in making up a plausible sounding story. The skill lies in showing readers how the facts will benefit them.

Let's use a consumer example, although the same theory applies to the business-to-business variety. This is the launch of a new window cleaning service. First, the wrong way.

Dear Sir

(First mistake. Many householders are women. It's also a bit too formal for this audience, and this service.)

We are proud to announce the new See-Through window cleaning service in the XXXtown area.

(Wrong again. You may be proud to announce it, but to say so sounds old-fashioned, pompous and affected. The reader doesn't care about you or whether you're proud or not.)

Our 20-strong team of cleaners has been fully trained to ensure an efficient and thorough service to householders...

(How many cleaners does it take to do the windows of the average home, unless you're talking the White House, Buckingham Palace, or the Sydney Opera House? One? Two, maybe? You may be impressed by your 20 star performers, but they'll make your readers think they're in for a large expense.)

... at very attractive, cost-effective rates.

(Nonsense, says the reader. Cost-effective is what businesses say when they try to justify high prices. I only react to facts. Like how much would it cost for an average three-bedroom townhouse?)

We also offer discounts to groups of 10 or more households wishing to have their windows cleaned at the same time.

(Where? Zimbabwe? Alaska? Halfway up the Andes? What about me and my neighbors?)

Further details of this discount facility are available on request.

(You'll tell me about prices if I ask you nicely. Nuts to that. I want to know now.)

If you would like more information on the new See-Through window cleaning service, please contact our office.

> (Well, at least you finally remembered who you were writing to. But why should I contact your office? And who? The canteen manager? And where? One of those funny little phone numbers at the bottom of the letterhead in six point type? If you want me to buy from you, make it easy.)

Yours faithfully

> (oh come on – you're not writing to a tax inspector!)

I. Glass Chairman

> (Gosh, a real chairman. I wonder how much he knows about how I like my windows cleaned. Haven't you got someone a bit more in touch with me and my needs?)

OK. Let's try again with a more appropriate style and approach, using headings to break up the text and emphasize key benefits. We also need to give far more in the way of facts.

Dear Householder,

A CLEAN, CLEAR VIEW FROM YOUR WINDOWS AT A COST THAT CLEARLY MAKES SENSE

Window cleaning can be a time-consuming chore for you – messy, dirty and even dangerous. Paying someone else to do it can help. But can you always rely on them to turn up regularly?

Now, though, you can leave the problem of window cleaning to us. See-Through window cleaners have just set up a new, professional service in your area... to clean your windows as often as you want, on a regular basis. All you have to do is tell us how often you want us – biweekly, monthly, three-monthly or whatever suits you best – and one of our fully trained cleaners will be there every time, on time.

And you don't pay more because we're professional. An average three-bedroom townhouse costs around YY.00. That's less than many independent casual window cleaners charge.

GET TOGETHER WITH YOUR NEIGHBOURS AND BRING THE COST DOWN EVEN MORE

For 10 or more homes on a regular basis, we'll give you a discount of 20%. That brings the cost of an average three-bedroom townhouse down to just XX.00. And 20 homes or more get a massive 50% off.

LET US GIVE YOU A FREE QUOTATION

Just mark and post the enclosed reply-paid card, or email us here: clarity@seethrough.com.uk

We'll get in touch right away to make an appointment for one of our specialists to visit your home and give you a free, no-quibbles quote.

And if your windows need attention urgently, call us now on our Hotline – 0123 456789. We'll get one of our team over to you within 72 hours, at no extra charge.

Let See-Through give you a cleaner, clearer view from your windows – at a cost that clearly makes sense.

Warm regards

CLARITY GLASS Customer Services Adviser

Brochure copy

Probably the most interesting thing about brochures nowadays is that they're seldom read in what we've come to know as the right order – as you would read a book. Just as people read magazines in dentists' waiting rooms or scan text online, they will flick through brochures and leaflets and stop to take a longer look at bits that grab their attention. Alternatively they'll flick all the way through and then go back to bits they've noticed and that have interested them.

What all this teaches us is that despite seeming logical, writing for brochures in the form of a story that starts at the beginning, goes through the middle and finishes at the end, is not necessarily the best way forward. Obviously you can't make every page stand alone with a message on it that says "in case you're flicking through backwards or only want to read this page, here's a summary of our corporate profile again". But there are some tricks you can use to get this random reading pattern to work a bit more effectively for you, rather than against you.

A lot depends on the type and style of brochure or leaflet you want to write, of course. In my experience, generally speaking the more specific the purpose of a brochure or leaflet the more likely readers are to read it properly and thoroughly. Where you get the worst random grasshopper reading is with the less specific documents like corporate or general overview brochures. So let's look at how we can minimize the problems with those.

Structure with cross headings

The trick is to put the main points in as crossheadings (some people call them sub-headings) in bold type, so that someone scanning the document will get the gist of your message even if they don't have time to read the body text. You should also ensure that the crossheadings make sense in their own right and that understanding them is not wholly dependent on their being read in any particular order.

Body text should be short, and should support and expand on each crossheading, leading the reader towards the next one, but without creating a "cliffhanger" (in case the reader is going in the wrong order).

Choose writing style carefully

The other key issue here is writing style, particularly if you are writing a corporate brochure or leaflet. The corporate brochure, equaled only (perhaps) by the corporate website, is the most prone to suffer from the curse of "corporate speak".

It's interesting to see that many companies find it easy to write in their audience's own language for advertisements and other marketing communications, but grind to a juddering halt when it comes to a corporate brochure. Why? I'm not sure, but I suspect it's connected with the long tradition of corporate brochures being written by or on behalf of Chairmen and other very, very senior wallahs who believed their immense importance could only be conveyed in words of five syllables or more.

In the real world, however, normal customers and other stakeholders find stuffy, pompous, remote brochure text boring and off-putting. So if they're your audience it's essential you write in a way that they will identify with.

No matter what the 70-year-old President thinks, it *is* possible to retain corporate dignity without using wall-to-wall multisyllabic words phrased entirely in terms of the "royal we".

Taglines

People argue about taglines although they have been around for years. They even argue about what they're called.

We've seen a variety of names starting with the delightfully old-fashioned "slogan", through to more modern terms like "strapline", "baseline", "endline", etc. Personally, I quite like "tagline."

However what matters is not what they're called, but what they are. People argue about that, too. My own view is that a tagline is a short phrase that supports a name or brand, bringing attention to what the name or brand does for the reader.

In some ways a tagline acts as a microscopic mission statement. Another way of putting it is to call it the opening line of your "value proposition".

Yes, it's quite an important little phrase. Particularly with a new project/product/service, it lays the foundation for how that will be perceived.

Developing taglines for major brands and branding exercises is a skilled job and probably not one that should be tackled by the uninitiated. Many different criteria creep into big brand stories and even the experts will spend a lot of money testing taglines, logos, etc before issuing them.

However, using taglines is not restricted to the Kelloggs and Coca Colas of this world. They are also useful for a variety of other, less global purposes. You may well find them useful to include as subtitles to the name of a project, proposal, report or other business document, by supporting the main title and adding gravitas to it.

So how do we approach creating a tagline?

Brainstorming

Many people tell you that the best way to set about creating a tagline is to brainstorm your way through a large selection of words and phrases that you randomly associate with your project. (By project I mean project/product/service, but I'm keeping it down to one word for the sake of brevity.)

They tell you to note down every word that comes into your mind which can be associated with your project. They tell you to look up as much as you can in the dictionary and the thesaurus. Write it all down. Have a word feast and sooner or later the bones of a good tagline will fall out.

Well, I agree with that up to a point. It can be useful. But to my way of thinking there is a shortcut you can take, and that amounts to a reality check.

As I suggested earlier, what really makes a good tagline is how it encapsulates what the project achieves for the intended audience.

So, when I'm attempting to create a tagline, that's what I look at first.

I say to myself, OK. What does this project really achieve – or intend to achieve – for its recipients? In other words, does it offer a key benefit?

Then I start writing down ideas that encapsulate that. Not what the project means to me, or to the client, or to the Board of Directors. What it means to the recipient of the project. What it will do for him/her. What its key benefit is. (I know, I keep harping on about focusing on benefits and "what's in it for them". But in business, what else is there to keep the wheels turning?)

And if you keep those thoughts firmly in your mind, suddenly you'll find you're writing tagline ideas that are much crisper, more focused, and more relevant.

How to handle too many benefits

A few years ago I was called in by a chain of estate agents (realtors) in the UK to help them develop their marketing message. I arrived to find half a dozen sweaty, harassed team members all working away on long lists of genuine benefits that their company offered customers. Many of those benefits were unique to the company, and their service offering truly was excellent.

However that was part of the problem; there were too many benefits. Despite hours of brainstorming they hadn't yet been able to see the wood for the trees. It was time for me to speak up.

Although my role here, as an external consultant, was to play "agent provocateur", you can do this yourself provided you can step away mentally from the brainstorming exercise.

"OK," I said. "Let's group all those benefits together for a moment. What do they achieve collectively for the customer? What is one of the biggest negatives about buying and selling your home? And how do we overcome that?"

Gradually, I saw some light bulbs switching on over people's heads. "Yes," I said as they all started smiling. "We take the stress out of it."

Not only did that get developed into a tagline – it also formed the basis of their value proposition over the ensuing months and was very successful.

The takeout point here, is stand back and look at the tagline from different angles. Brainstorm your benefits, then ask yourselves what those benefits achieve collectively. I know this is an awful cliché, but "think outside the box".

Some examples and more tips

Let's look at a few examples now. First, the self-indulgent, zero-benefit variety that sadly you still see today;

- **"We're no 1"**

- **"The tastiest pizzas in town"**
- **"First for XXX software"**

As we've seen, a tagline needs to be developed on the basis of what is achieved for the recipient by the name or brand the tagline supports. To do this it needs not only to say what you want recipients to believe, but also why they should believe it.

So how about, **"We're no 1 because we work harder for you"**? If you must say you're no 1 at anything, don't expect anyone to believe it unless there's some sort of justification.

How about **"pizzas that turn on your taste buds"** ? If you say "the tastiest" it's tempting to reply, "says who?" This version, then, makes it clear for whom the benefit is intended.

And how about **"first for XXX software that grows your business – not your costs"**? Once again, an upfront benefit that justifies and qualifies your "first" status.

Finally, there's the issue of sound and rhythm in a tagline. Even if it isn't destined to be spoken or sung in a TV commercial, a tagline that "sounds" attractive will be more easily remembered than one which uses awkward words and construction, no matter how accurate.

By all means use the literary tricks of alliteration and assonance, even rhymes if the topic is fairly light-hearted. Use "active voice", not passive voice. Use short words rather than long ones, and keep adjectives and adverbs to a minimum.

If you'd like to read more about creating taglines and see some live examples, you'll find some good ones on the *Marketing Professionals Know-How Exchange.*

I'm one of the regular contributors, so you're likely to see my suggestions crop up regularly! To get into the forum you may need to register, but at that level it's FOC and I promise, you won't get spammed. It's well worth a look.

Product copy

Many people fail to realize that product copy should be well crafted. Often their objective in creating a printed catalogue or catalogue-style website is to cram in as many products as they can, with descriptive copy kept to a few mis-spelled words in tiny type squashed into a corner. These people are the on-paper equivalent of the "stack 'em high, sell 'em cheap" species you encounter in retailing.

However, in a retail environment customers can usually pick up the products, have a good look at them, read the on-pack copy and find out all they need to know. So the fact that they're in a no-frills environment doesn't matter too much. When a product is pictured in the small, two-dimensional environment of the printed page or computer screen it's not only no-frills but also very lonely, unless the product has the support of some well-chosen words to inform readers and encourage them to buy it.

Considering that for many organizations their printed catalogue and/or catalogue-style website is their only shop window – or at least represents, potentially, a very significant revenue stream – you would think that everyone's attention and skill would be focused on its written content as much as its other elements. But no. All too often this type of product copy looks as though it has been written by a monosyllabic eight-year-old who was busy playing a computer game at the same time.

What do you need to say?
Some products that get sold "off the page" or "off the screen" do not need a lot of description and the only words you need to include are choice of colours/sizes/quantities etc. However there is always the temptation to use the product copy space, however small, to inject a bit of sales impetus in addition to the factual information.

Although a little sales nudge here and there is no bad thing, a catalogue or website in which every block of product copy text is loaded with glowing adjectives gets boring to read and loses a lot of impact. Quite apart from the fact that finding umpty-dump different ways to describe computer printers or sports clothes is very difficult, even for pro writers like me, it also lacks credibility.

Current marketing trends recognize that the buyers, whether consumer, B2B, technical or otherwise, have become fed up with being overtly sold to over and over again. Of course, much depends on the nature of the product you're selling, but in my experience, whatever the product type, what potential buyers want today is good, clear, thorough information. And anything but the occasional product eulogy merely irritates them and puts them off.

"How to order" messages

I don't know about you, but if I'm thinking of buying something from a printed catalogue or catalogue-style website, there's nothing that puts me off faster than having to spend a lot of time figuring out how to fill out the form, work out what's in my shopping cart, where the checkout is, how to pay, etc .

It's not difficult to get the process right. Simply work out the steps you want customers to take, write them down simply, and then try them out on your mother, your brother, your neighbor, a college professor, the milkman, or anyone else – provided they are not involved with your organization. That's a cheap and fast way of discovering any flaws in the system, especially small goofs that can get overlooked so easily if you're too familiar with them.

Beware of including too much information on catalogue or website ordering pages. It's very laudable to supply as much information as you can to help your customers arrive at their buying decision. However you don't want to stuff so many facts and figures into their faces on a single page or screen that they fail to spot the "sign here" or "submit" slots.

Keep the ordering process as simple and straightforward as you can. Put the additional-but-non-critical details somewhere else and refer customers to them if they want to look at them separately.

And here's another one, fortunately pertaining to printed catalogues only. How many times have you looked at a catalogue only to find that crucial information you should keep (like contact details for ordering, delivery information, etc) is placed either on the order form itself or on the back of the page the order form is on?

The result is, when you mail off your completed order form you're obliged to mail that important information away with it. Stupid, huh? At least with websites you don't have that problem.

Keep it crisp and focused

There is no mystery about creating good product copy for catalogues and websites – only common sense. It's perfectly OK in my view to keep your writing crisp and concise because it helps to use the space more efficiently.

But whatever you do, never lose sight of the fact that the way this text is written and designed says a lot more about your organization than you think. If it is cluttered, unclear and illogical, customers will think your company is too. If it is busy but accessible, clear and easy to understand and logically planned, well – need I say more?

Retailers spend fortunes on the design, layout and flow of their instore displays. Supermarkets can increase or decrease their turnover by thousands, simply by moving the fresh produce from the back wall to the side wall or by putting the bakery beyond the delicatessen or by increasing the aisle width by a few centimeters.

Think of your catalogue/website as a paper-/screen-based store or supermarket, and you'll find it easier to give it the consideration and respect it deserves.

General business

Writing about yourself

BEFORE YOU DO ANYTHING ELSE, ask yourself not what you want to say, but what you want to achieve with the text. Be honest with yourself and don't be overly ambitious. Once you've clearly identified your objective, keep it in mind throughout the writing exercise. You'll find that keeps you on track far more effectively – what you want to achieve should define what you say.

Modesty has no place here

Forget modesty. As an experienced salesperson would say, "If you don't think you're good, why the h*ll should I?" Equally, of course, you don't want to exaggerate your strengths – that can lead to problems when you're eventually called upon to deliver! But be realistic about what you can do and don't be afraid to describe it in a positive light.

A useful way to achieve that is to step outside yourself and regard yourself as a product or better still, as a brand. For the purposes of this exercise you are not Mary Doe the person. You are writing about Mary Doe the brand. It's not as difficult as it sounds; write in the third person to start with, if you find that more comfortable. Imagine you're a colleague writing about you. If required you can change it back to the first person later.

What do you do for your reader?

Bear in mind that whoever reads this text probably won't care much about you; they'll only care about what you can do for them. Structure everything with that in mind. If you need to include factual/statistical information (educational details, qualifications, etc) then make sure you put it in a box so it's visually separated from the main text.

Where possible, identify the audience who will be reading your text and aim your writing squarely at them. It's possible that the "core" of your text can remain the same for a number of different purposes, with individual "tops and tails" aimed at specific audiences. The more relevant your text is to the reader – telling him/her how you and your service meet their needs – the more successful the text will be.

Write realistically, and for real

First person or third person? Earlier on –I suggested that you write in the third person to make it easier for you to regard yourself in an objective light. However there are times when you may need to present your text in the first person – e.g. in a letter or email. Writing in the first person is more intimate and can come across as more truthful and "from the heart". Writing in the third person is harder and more commercial. If you have the choice, make it on the basis of who will be reading your text, and why.

Where appropriate, use short clips of testimonials from existing clients or customers. Avoid the pleasantly banal bits and use phrases and sentences that have some meaning and bite. A sentence or two normally is plenty – any more and the reader will probably just skim over it.

Get the nuts and bolts right and do a reality check

Be sure that your grammar, spelling and punctuation are right. Although standards have been slipping in the last few years, the publication of the book *Eats, Shoots and Leaves* has focused everyone's attention on the technical aspects of writing again. Goofs of this nature make your text, and you, look amateurish.

Do a reality check on your text after you've completed it. Show it to friends and colleagues and ask not if they "like" it, but if they feel it represents you fairly – and if not, why not. Then take other people's opinions on board, but don't lose sleep over them. You probably know yourself, and your market, better than anyone else. Don't be afraid to make final judgments.

For a detailed look at this topic, along with many more tips, examples, guidelines, and other useful information, you'll find my eBook, *How To Sell Yourself In Writing*, very helpful. It covers:

http://howtowritebetter.net/must-have-books/

- "About Us" pages for your business
- Personal "about" pages/bios/profiles
- CVs/résumés
- Covering letters and emails
- Personal statements (university)
- Personal statements (CVs/résumés)
- Getting good testimonials
- Your personal brand
- Personal blogging
- Autobiographies

Business documents

Although any form of business writing should be benefits-led, with business documents and proposals it often doesn't pay to be too blatant about "what's in it for them". Heading such a document, "Back my suggestions for a new company gymnasium and your promotion prospects could be enhanced" might be true, but you won't score many points by rubbing readers' noses in the fact. Benefits to the reader should be strongly implied rather than spelled out.

Some business documents and proposals need to follow set formats – either those of your own organization, or those decreed by etiquette like, for example, business plans in the UK. Even with the latter category, the etiquette for which was developed by bankers and accountants and management consultants and other noble professionals not normally known for their creative writing skills, you can still write in a way that grabs and holds readers' attention. The trick is not to be intimidated by the formality of such formats. By all means stick to the defined sequence and format, but that needn't stop you writing simple, clear stuff that's benefits led.

Another key issue with business documents and proposals is getting the structure right. Assuming you don't have a set format to follow and you can choose your own way forward, it's worth remembering that some if not all of the people who will read your document haven't got much time to spare. Even if they have, they're likely to want to move swiftly on from a business document to the sports page of the newspaper or an e-mail from a friend. So no matter how much detail you and your colleagues feel should be included to substantiate your document, keep that in the back (in appendices) and focus the front on the key points. In fact, try to get the key points of the whole story into one page, using subsequent pages for expansion. Your readers will be grateful to obtain the gist of your proposition quickly and, assuming the rest of it makes good sense, that will place you in the front line for a "yes".

Go with the flow

Staying with the structure issue, it's also important to work out the flow of the content so that your information and your argument are presented in a logical way. This is not as challenging as it sounds. Once again, assuming you're not obliged to follow set procedures, it pays to forget whatever old-fashioned precedents may exist and trust your instincts. Provided that you have informed yourself thoroughly about the people who will be reading your document, your instincts will tell you what they will want to know, what elements of it will really ring their chimes, and in what order. If the audience is diverse (e.g. some management, some finance, some technical) you can attach their individual categories of detail as appendices, keeping the central flow of the document focused on the main issues that are common to all. That makes it much more powerful.

Readers are human, whoever they are – and they're busy

Always remember that no matter how faceless and terrifying you imagine business angels or venture capitalists or senior bank executives might be, they're all human beings who react in a human way to human words.

In fact, if anything, they will warm to good, clear, strong, human writing (provided the proposition itself is valid) rather more than they will to the long-winded, boring, stuffy prose they probably have to wade through in 95% of cases.

Be natural and informal

And finally, whatever you do, don't think that because you're writing a business document the style has to be dry, dull and boring. Especially if you know the people who will be reading it (but even if you don't), be informal and use friendly, natural language. My old boss years ago – one of the best direct mail copywriters the UK has ever seen – used to say that the right tone of voice for good sales copy is as if you were standing next to the reader, chatting to him or her in a pub. With business documents I suppose we should forget the pub, but I believe they should be written in the same tone of voice as if you were talking to the reader over a cup of coffee at an informal meeting.

One of the great advantages of written communication is that people don't have to live up to their external images when they're reading it. Even if they're pompous, conceited bigots in company, when they're alone they're just like you and me. That means they are likely to respond better, in private, to informal, straightforward, honest words than they are – ironically – to the sort of elaborate garbage they themselves speak and write to others. It helps to remember that point when you're writing anything for business, and especially when you're writing in a politically upwards rather than sideways or downwards direction.

Business letters

Many people in business heaved a sigh of relief when email began to take over most of their day-to-day correspondence. Processing business letters – even today – is fiddly and fussy, compared with the blissful simplicity of email.

However, as you know, there are still times when ink on paper is essential. Many of the so-called "professions" (legal, accountancy, etc), still insist on correspondence being done via printed letters. They have a deep mistrust of email and for good reason, as its confidentiality can never be guaranteed. Business letters are at least fairly private; you have to assume it's easier and faster to snoop on email than it is to steam envelopes open over boiling water.

In other instances, too, printed letters provide a more tamper-proof formal record of business arrangements, complaints, employee warnings/ terminations and other issues that need to be carved into tablets of stone (well, paper, anyway).

Old fashioned structure, modern style

Highlighted and ridiculed by the casual nature of email, the quaint formality of the old fashioned business letter seems positively Dickensian and totally inappropriate for the way we do business now.

There is an answer, though. Use the formality of structure that makes the business letter the bullet-proof form of communication it has come to be. Combine that with the short, straight-talking style of writing more common to emails, and you have a good compromise.

Let's start with the structure – or rather, the etiquette which supplies the structure.

There are variations between accepted etiquette used in the different English language markets. Here are the main British and US/Canadian forms of address (I'm afraid I'm not aware of those used in Australia, NZ or SA):

Formal letters

The addressee will either be a title, e.g. "The Chief Executive Officer", or to an organization or company when you don't know to whom your letter should be addressed. When you write to a title the salutation is "Dear Sir", "Dear Madam", or if you want to play it safe, "Dear Sir/Madam". When you write to an organization it's "Dear Sirs", Dear "Mesdames", or again, if you want to play it safe (but labor the point), "Dear Sirs/Mesdames".

Your sign off will be "Yours truly" (US and Canada) or "Yours faithfully" (UK).

Less formal letters

This is where you have a name. And this is where you can get into hot water if you're not sure of the gender of the person. Someone called J C Jennings could be a Jack or a Joanna. Someone called Leslie Matthews could also be either (traditionally the female version of the name is spelled "Lesley" and the male "Leslie", but I know at least one woman Leslie.)

Equally beware of unisex names like Jody/Jodie, Jo/Joe, Bobbie/Bobby, Alex, Rob, Robin/Robyn, Carol, Evelyn (yes, really), Billie, Chris, Darryl, Eddie, Sam, Jackie, Nicky/Nikki, Frances (f) vs Francis (m), Freddie, Gabrielle (f) vs Gabriel (m), Georgie, Gerry/Jerry, Charlie, Nat, Harry, Jessie (f) vs Jesse (m), Stevie, Mel, Pat, Ronnie, Sacha, Sandy, etc. And that's before we get started on names from non English-language cultures.

People these days usually don't advertise whether they're "Mr", "Ms" or whatever. When in doubt, don't risk embarrassment; phone the organization concerned and ask.

Some people borrow an awful technique from email and use a person's whole name in the salutation, e.g.

"Dear Suzan St Maur". I don't know about you, but this irritates the h*ll out of me and I would not recommend it.

So, when your letter is addressed to "Mr J. C. Jennings" your salutation is "Dear Mr Jennings". If the information you have is simply "Joanna C. Jennings", you can probably take a chance and write a salutation of "Dear Ms Jennings". I don't know any male Joannas, but don't take my word for it...

Your sign off will be "Yours sincerely".

Even less formal letters

This is where the internet's influence can be allowed to come in and give you some freedom from the formalities expected in, well, more formal letters.

If you're writing to someone whom you know on first name terms, your salutation is going to be "Dear (name)" and you don't need to sign off with a "yours" anything unless you particularly want to. Common forms of sign off include "warm regards" (US), "kind regards", "best wishes", etc.

Layout

This isn't as strictly followed as it used to be, and now it's considered OK to design the layout of a letter around the design of the company letterhead. The elements you need, wherever you put them, should include:

- Your company name and address (usually done in the letterhead's design)

- The date
- The addressee's name, title, company name and address
- The salutation ("dear so-and-so")
- The topic of the letter ("re:" whatever)
- The body of the letter
- The sign off ("Yours whatever")
- Your own name and title

Traditionally, your own address should go at the top right of the letter, with the date underneath it on the right. On the next line, at the left margin, you put the addressee's name and address. The "Dear (whoever)" goes underneath that after one or two spaces. Two spaces below that, you can put your "re: (topic)" or just the topic in bold and/or underlined.

Once you've written the body of the letter, create one or two spaces and put the sign-off, either ranged left or indented a few tabs along towards the right. Create a sufficient number of spaces for your signature and then key in your name (and title if appropriate) so it starts directly under the "Y" of "Yours".

If your letter goes on to a second page, where it breaks on page one, create a space underneath to the right, and key in "cont'd". You can start page two just by keying in "page 2" and starting again two or three spaces below. Some people create a mini-heading for the second page with the addressee's name on the left, the date in the middle, and the page number on the right, followed by an underline that crosses the whole page. This is useful if the two pages become detached from one another.

OK. Now we've established the ground rules, what do we say?

Keep the style sharp and simple

Business letters are not a literary art form. They are verbal workhorses with the purpose of only conveying information, and what you want the reader to do with it, as quickly and clearly as possible.

Start by making notes as if to yourself. These notes will come out in a direct style naturally, because you're not intimidated or disquieted when writing to yourself. Don't restrict yourself to a structure at this stage. Just write out everything you can think of that should go into the letter.

Now, match your notes to the sequence in one of the "skeletons" described below. Discard any notes that aren't relevant.

If you build up your letter along these lines you'll find that your style is clear and straightforward, with no unnecessary adjectives, adverbs, business phrases, "corporate speak" or other business BS that some people use in business letters.

All you need to do then is tidy up with a good edit and

spelling and grammar check. (Although many people take a lenient view over spelling and grammatical mistakes in emails, they stick out like sore thumbs in printed letters and make you look very amateurish.)

Build your content on a "skeleton"

Normally you'll identify the topic of the letter with "re: Your Outstanding Account" or less formally, "Your Outstanding Account" in bold and/or underlined. Then make notes or bullet points of the main issues you need to include, on a skeleton like the one shown below.

Typically, these bullet points might be:

1. Background

I see from our records that you were first invoiced for this amount four months ago and statements have been sent out to you each month since then.

2. The sticky issue

This can't go on, especially as you haven't contacted us to discuss extending your credit.

3. What I want to happen now

Pay up in the next seven days.

4. Or else

We will be obliged to start legal proceedings against you.

5. Sweetener

If you do pay up by return, we won't take any further action and will restart your 30 days' credit as before.

6. Next move

Please contact me urgently and let me know what you intend to do.

Same skeleton, different content

You could use this skeleton for a number of business letter purposes. Not all business letters have you sitting so comfortably in the driving seat, however. Let's say you were the recipient of this letter and want to winkle out more time to pay. The elements remain the same, but we approach from a different angle...

1. Background

Thank you for bringing this to my attention – I had no idea we were so late paying.

2. The sticky issue

We're experiencing serious cash flow problems at the moment, but we have taken steps to rectify this and anticipate the problem will be solved in the next three weeks.

3. What I want to happen now

Would you consider extending our credit for a while longer, perhaps with interest being chargeable at a rate we can agree?

4. Or else

We really would like to continue buying our supplies from you, but if we enter into a dispute the goodwill will be lost and our business relationship will be over.

5. Sweetener

I can assure you our cash flow problem is temporary and we want to preserve our business relationship with you if possible.

6. Next move

I will phone you in the next few days to discuss payment terms.

Build your own skeleton

Obviously that six-point skeleton isn't going to work for every business letter, but a shortened version of it will be useful because you can build it back up so it's tailored to any number of different needs. Here's the basic one that I use:

1. Background
2. The key issue
3. What will or should happen
4. What to do next

Any further tips?

Only that business letters should always be as short as possible. That's not as simple as it sounds. Remember that old quote which has been around for generations and attributed to several *men of letters:* "**So sorry only to write you a long letter, but I did not have the time to write you a short one.**" What this means is that it's hard to write concisely, but if you use the style and skeleton tips above you'll find it somewhat easier.

If you need to go into detail, separate that off into a different (but attached) document and use the letter only as a summary of the issue and a call to action.

I'm no social psychologist so I can't quote you a scientific reason, but separating detail from key points usually means that both get read more thoroughly. It's probably because by separating the two elements you provide readers with more digestible looking chunks. Anyway, it works!

Proposals

Rather than spout theory at you yet again, I've taken an example I used in one of my books, Powerwriting, and reworked it for us here. As storytelling is such a popular way of conveying business messages these days, this is the story of a catering manager who wants the Board to fund a "tasty" new kitchen.

The scenario
You are the catering manager of a large company. You're responsible for a team of 20 staff who cook and serve subsidized canteen lunches for the

workforce of 500 people. The equipment in your kitchen is 10 years old and pretty worn out. Your kitchen staff are unhappy about this and are forever complaining. You decide to put some proposals together to convince the Board (your direct report is the HR VP or Director) to allocate funds for new equipment. This is how you might go about thinking through your writing project, making notes as you go – but not writing it yet.

1. What is my desired outcome – that I should keep in my mind at all times?

Obtain available funds to buy and install new kitchen equipment for the staff restaurant.

2. What secondary objectives do I have?

It would be nice to have carte blanche to spend the money how I like and buy what equipment I want without having to justify every last penny/dime/sou to the financial people. To achieve this and equip the kitchen appropriately would:

- Improve my relationship with my staff and ease my conscience about their need to work with out-dated and slow equipment
- Stop the stream of complaints from the workforce when they have to wait for their food longer than is reasonable – which wastes my time as I have to listen to them and deal with them

- Ultimately reduce my costs through more efficient energy usage and faster turnaround
- Create happier employees, which will make me look better to my superiors

3. So what exactly is needed to achieve these outcomes?

I need to produce a short, sharp and convincing document that Board members will read during the week prior to the next meeting. The HR VP/Director has promised me that he will include it as an item in his section of the tabled agenda. I've only got one shot, so it had better be good.

4. Who are the people in my "audience" and what does it feel like to be them?

They're senior executives who seldom eat in the staff restaurant, so the issue is unlikely to be of personal importance to them. They are likely to feel stressed at the moment because of recent rumours about a hostile takeover bid from one of our competitors. Sales have been down a bit lately and so they're likely to be in the mood for cost cutting.

The last time someone applied for money to be spent on staff facilities they actually were very generous and sanctioned funds for a complete refit of the restaurant itself, and that was just last year. They may not be in the mood to spend almost as much again, especially as the kitchen facilities are not visible to them, to visitors and to the vast majority of staff, so they won't perceive much PR value.

However the HR Director is going to discuss a major recruitment problem at the Board meeting and all Board members are going to be made aware that we are losing much in the way of local work skills and talent to our competitors in the next town. This is partly because of their superior training schemes and personal development programmes, but also it is due to their superior staff perks, including a superb restaurant and gymnasium.

5. How will the audience receive my message?

In the form of a document along with a stack of other documents one week prior to the meeting, probably lumped together in one file or binder. They're likely to be pressed for time so will probably skim all documents while travelling by train/plane/chauffeur-driven car, or maybe at home at the weekend or late at night in a hotel room somewhere.

In the meeting the topic will be flagged up by the HR Director, but this will be secondary to the recruitment problem and in any case the whole HR section is likely to be quite a long way down the agenda. The executives are likely to be tired and grumpy by this time, especially if earlier news has not been good. It may be possible to put a summary of my message on the Board level company intranet, which, if it's read at all, will be read after the document has been circulated but before the Board meeting.

6. What's in it for them – what benefits are there for my audience?

In this case, more than in most, I've got to sing out a benefit for the recipients of my message so fast it isn't funny, otherwise the whole thing will be shuffled to the bottom of the deck and may not even get discussed at the Board meeting. What could possibly be in it for the Board, as they don't even eat in the staff restaurant? Hang on... the competition in the next town recruiting staff on the basis of a better deal including a brilliant staff restaurant. That's going to be discussed before my project. Now we're getting somewhere...

7. How can I make the negatives look as un-negative as possible?

The cost. Yup. Tricky. I can hear them now saying, "But only last year we paid to have the whole restaurant refitted, and now we're being asked for more?" But supposing that was step one? Hmmm.

How about this? A heading that reads something like... "Maximising staff satisfaction – our final step in gaining the lead as local recruiters" – yes! I like it.

That's the angle to use: I've got to show them how investing in new kitchen equipment will help put us in a much stronger staff retention and recruitment position and, as such, is a particularly relevant issue for consideration now when our competitors are threatening to take the best of the local workforce for themselves.

8. Have I genuinely demonstrated that there's something "in it" for everyone?

Yes. And there's nothing dishonest about it; the point I'm making is absolutely true. It's just that from where I sit, I wouldn't necessarily have looked at it that way, and it was only by putting myself into the audience's shoes that I looked at it from another direction.

The final proposal...

Page 1 / cover

> **Inhouse catering – the final step: ...crucial to secure staff satisfaction and maximize the benefits of last year's restaurant refit**
>
> *How a relatively modest investment in new kitchen equipment will complete our excellent inhouse catering service ...*
>
> *... and ensure it earns its keep as a significant staff benefit that's better than anything our competitors offer their employees*

Page 2

The immediate problem

Last year saw the refurbishment of our staff restaurant, which has gone some way towards making our inhouse catering service the best of any employer in the city. However, equipment "behind the scenes" in the kitchens themselves, has not been replaced since 200X. This old equipment is slow and laborious to use – even by our highly trained and well-motivated kitchen staff – which results in frequent, lengthy delays in delivering food orders to diners in the restaurant. Consequent dissatisfaction among restaurant users is on the increase, especially in view of our recent productivity and sales drive, which has led to shorter lunch breaks and resultant pressure for orders to materialize faster – not slower.

The secondary problems

At a time when Bozo Ltd are featuring their staff facilities as a major incentive for people to join their organization, the last thing we need is for our staff catering service to let us down and make our company less attractive. Last year's investment in improving the "front of house" restaurant fittings made a substantial contribution towards putting things right, but without modern kitchen equipment to keep up the pace, those restaurant *fittings can't do the job on their own. Also, there is now a risk that our old kitchen equipment may fail to meet current health, safety and hygiene requirements which would necessitate replacement in any case before too long.*

The solution

Compared with what was spent last year on restaurant refurbishment, what's needed now for kitchen equipment is actually less, though its effect will be, if anything, more valuable. This is because the spend on new equipment will lead to a huge overall improvement in service – important for our staff recruitment/retention.

Implementation

As you will see overleaf, I have conducted an exhaustive cost/performance comparison survey of all appropriate equipment. Based on my long experience of industrial kitchen management I have made detailed recommendations for the most cost-effective choices. I am also happy to oversee the purchase and installation of the equipment personally, to save on management time within the Purchasing and Finance departments and to ensure the most efficient overall solution.

The outcome

Updating our staff restaurant kitchen equipment will be the final link in the chain of ensuring our staff facilities not only meet, but excel those of Bozo Ltd and any other local organizations seeking to attract high-calibre staff. As you know, often it is these relatively small issues – and these relatively small investments – which tip the scales in favour of a star recruit's decision to join one organization or the other. We want them to join and stay with ours, and this initiative will help ensure that they do.

Page 3-4

How much will it cost?

(details of equipment required and costs thereof)

What it will achieve?

(cooking/serving time reduction, also energy usage reduction, etc)

Implementation plan

(what needs to be bought now, how/when it would be installed)

Outcomes measurement

(how soon improvements could be measured, what would be anticipated, staff satisfaction survey prospects, etc)

And the post-mortem...

First of all, consider the style and tone of voice. We are direct and to-the-point and do not use flowery or formal language, but at the same time we are not familiar or chatty. This is straight business-speak with no frills, to get our message over as effectively as possible in the shortest possible time while providing them with enough information to understand the whole issue.

Page 1 / cover

Inhouse catering – the final step:
...crucial to secure staff satisfaction and
maximize the benefits of last year's restaurant refit

This acts like a headline and has to flag up the key points of "what's in it for them", which, particularly in this case, is quite different from what's in it for me, the catering manager, and even for the staff who will benefit from it. As the message brief defined it, there are two key pressure points for the audience – one, attracting and retaining staff in the face of growing competition and two, the fact that last year they already spent quite a lot on the restaurant. This latter point could easily be used by them as an excuse not to contemplate this extra spend, which is why I've made such a fuss about the kitchen equipment being the "final link in the chain", almost hinting that it was their deliberate policy to refit the catering operation in two stages, this being the second.

How a relatively modest investment in new kitchen equipment will complete our excellent inhouse catering service ... and ensure it earns its keep as a significant staff benefit that's better than anything our competitors offer their employees

Relatively modest means little, but it sounds low. We're also hinting strongly that without new kitchen equipment the restaurant refit might have been a waste of money, which is probably true, but it wouldn't be very tactful of us to spell it out.

Page 2
The immediate problem
Last year saw the refurbishment of our staff restaurant which has gone some way towards making our inhouse catering service the best of any employer in the city. However equipment "behind the scenes" in the kitchens themselves, has not been

replaced since 200X. This old equipment is slow and laborious to use – even by our highly trained and well-motivated kitchen staff – which results in frequent, lengthy delays in delivering food orders to diners in the restaurant. Consequent dissatisfaction among restaurant users is on the increase, especially in view of our recent productivity and sales drive which has led to shorter lunch breaks and resultant pressure for orders to materialize faster – not slower.

Self-explanatory, really. Also, note that I anticipated another potential "get-out clause" for someone not wishing to sanction the spend – that it's not the age of the equipment that causes delays, but the inability/sloth of the kitchen staff. The sentence above might not convince them that the kitchen staff are superb, but it shows I've anticipated that possible objection and will fight it if it gets brought up. Often that's enough to stop such an objection in its tracks.

The secondary problems

At a time when Bozo Ltd are featuring their staff facilities as a major incentive for people to join their organization, the last thing we need is for our staff catering service to let us down and make our company less attractive. Last year's investment in improving the "front of house" restaurant fittings made a substantial contribution towards putting things right, but without modern kitchen equipment to keep up the pace those restaurant fittings can't do the job on their own. Also, there is now a risk that our old kitchen equipment may fail to meet current health, safety and hygiene requirements which would necessitate replacement in any case before too long.

Here I substantiate and reinforce the notion that the refit of the restaurant was stage one of a two-part project, that my stage two – re-equipping the kitchen – is necessary to complete the picture and, if it doesn't happen, could have dire consequences regarding our efforts to attract and retain good staff. Despite the new restaurant fittings.

The solution

Compared with what was spent last year on restaurant refurbishment, what's needed now for kitchen equipment is actually less, though its effect will be, if anything, more valuable. This is because the spend on new equipment will lead to a huge overall improvement in service – important for our staff recruitment/retention.

If this were a sales document it would be the "final push" section. However, with a document like this, once you've established your objective, which we have here (earlier on), this solution section acts more as a bridge and offers us the chance to remind the audience how what we want them to do relates to a benefit for them.

Implementation

As you will see overleaf, I have conducted an exhaustive cost/performance comparison survey of all appropriate equipment. Based on my long experience of industrial kitchen management I have made detailed recommendations for the most cost-effective choices. I am also happy to oversee the purchase and installation of the equipment personally, to save on management time within the Purchasing and Finance departments and to ensure the most efficient overall solution.

This section covers my "secondary considerations" from my message brief, whereby I would like to have carte blanche to organize the whole thing without other departments and managers breathing down my neck. Having searched high and low for a possible benefit to the Board, I realize that there's no better benefit than my own long experience as an expert in this area, and my considerate desire to save on others' management time by overseeing the project myself. Actually, it's win-win for everyone: I get to run the project as I think best and they don't have to wear the additional time and effort.

The outcome

Updating our staff restaurant kitchen equipment will be the final link in the chain of ensuring our staff facilities not only meet, but excel those of Bozo Ltd and any other local organizations seeking to attract high-calibre staff. As you know, often it is these relatively small issues – and these relatively small investments – which tip the scales in favour of a star recruit's decision to join one organization, or the other. We want them to join and stay with ours, and this initiative will help ensure that they do.

Really this is just a wishful-thinking summary, but it serves the purpose of wrapping up the main page and reminding the audience of the key points/potential benefits for them. The "as you know" phrase, provided it's used in a respectful rather than patronising way, can hint at a sort of conspiratorial partnership between writer and reader which can get the reader's head nodding up and down in silent agreement – always a usefully positive precursor to potential agreement.

Reports

There is one key difference between reports and most other forms of business writing, and we get a hint of that in the word, "report". Whereas with many other forms of written comms you can be a little creative and put your own slant on your words, in a report you must not. Not in theory, anyway.

In a report, you're supposed to report – not embellish, embroider, influence, etc. Just the facts and nothing but the facts.

This does not, however, mean that reports need to be dull and boring. It does, however, mean that you can't make the content interesting. Impossible? No, it just takes some good organization and clear writing.

Before we go any further, there are numerous books and training courses on the market that teach you the formalities and practicalities of report writing. Some are more long-winded than others. Most of them are good.

If you work in a larger organization, there will probably be set formats for reports, at least for the internal variety. Whether you like them or not you're normally obliged to stick to them. However, the way you roll out and write your content is still up to you.

So what are the key points to focus on?

1. Write for your reader

Don't allow yourself to fall into "businessese" jargon and phrasing, no matter how much you or other people may feel it's more appropriate. It isn't. Use language and tone of voice that your key readers will feel comfortable with. If you don't know what they feel comfortable with, find out. It's well worth taking the trouble, because it will make the report much more enjoyable for them to read – a good reflection on you.

If your report is to be read by a wide variety of different audiences, focus your language on the most important groups. Ensure that less topic-literate readers are catered for by using discreet explanations of technical terms or perhaps a short glossary of terms as an appendix within the report.

2. Organize your information sensibly

Start by writing yourself out a list of headings which start at the beginning and finish with the conclusions of your information. If you must include a lot of background information before you get into the "meat" of the information, section it off clearly with headings that say that it's background ("Research Project Objectives", "Research Methods Used To Collate Information", "Personnel Involved In Questionnaire" etc) so those who know it all already can skip straight to the important stuff.

Make sure your headings "tell the story" so someone glancing through those alone will get the basic messages. (You'll find that busy executives will thank you for doing this, especially when they have 16 other, similar reports to read in a crowded commuter train on the way into a meeting to discuss all of them.) Then fill in the details under each heading as concisely as you can.

3. Use an "executive summary" to tell it in a nutshell

Depending on the nature of your report, you may be expected to include an executive summary, or at least an introduction that captures the key points of your information. The objective of this is to give the reader the key issues as quickly as possible. Write this after you've done the body of the report, not before. Use your list of headings as a guide.

Keep strictly to the facts – this is still part of the report, not your interpretation of it. Strip each sentence down to bare bones with minimal adjectives and adverbs. Use short words and sentences. Don't just get to the point – start with it and stick to it.

4. If your interpretation is called for, keep it separate

If part of your remit is to comment on the report and/or its conclusions, keep this separate from the main body of information (blocked off in a box or under a clearly separated heading will do).

Naturally, as you're professional, you will be as objective as possible. But if you do feel strongly one way or another, ensure that your argument is put as reasonably as possible without going on for pages and pages. Remember, brief is beautiful, although it's harder to write briefly (and include all the important points) than it is to produce words in abundance.

5. Don't get carried away with illustrations

Graphs and charts are great to illustrate important issues and, like the man said, "a picture is worth a thousand words". However, ensure that those you use are of a level of complexity that will be understood by the least topic-literate of your readers. There's nothing more irritating than a graph that takes you 20 minutes to decipher. It's not so much a case that readers are too stupid to understand a complex graph as it is that they don't want to spend too much time working it out. The easier/quicker you make it for readers to understand and assimilate your information, the more successful your report.

Try, also, to keep graphs and charts physically adjacent to the text that talks about the same thing. There's nothing more irritating for the reader if they have to keep flipping from front to back of a document. (When in doubt, think of someone reading your report on a crowded commuter train.)

6. Cut the clutter

Still on that topic, try to avoid including too many diverse elements in your report, no matter how long and involved it is. If you do need to include appendices and various bits of background material, research statistics, etc, make sure they're neatly labeled and contained at the back of your document.

Don't ask readers to skip back and forth, directing them with asterisks and other reference directing symbols. If you're writing a medical/scientific/academic report or paper, I know you're obliged to include them when quoting references from other papers. However unless you are legally or professionally obliged to include a full trolley of references please keep these to a minimum, and preferably box them off in a list at the end of your report rather than clutter the main text with them. They're very distracting and can break your reader's concentration.

7. Take some trouble to make it look nice

I know you shouldn't judge a book by its cover, but people do. Like it or not. According to one image consultant I know, when you walk into a meeting, 55% of your first impression of someone is reflected exclusively in the way they're dressed. Documents fall into the same hole. So how your document looks goes a long way to creating the right impression of your work, and of you.

Obviously if a report is due to go outside your organization and particularly to clients or customers, you will be careful to ensure it's polished and clearly branded with your corporate identity and all that. However, how an internal report looks is important, too, although your Head of Finance might have apoplexy if you bind it in expensive glossy card. Be sensible with the internal variety – neat, understated, groomed looks don't have to cost much but they "say" a lot about the value of your report (and you.)

8. A minute on minutes

I think minute-taking is a horrible job, having done it for six years while on a charity fundraising committee. And being useless at handwriting (thanks to decades of computers and typewriters) never mind shorthand (was thrown out of secretarial school after three weeks) I struggled for months to scribble everything down to précis later, until I realized that my brain was a far more efficient filter of information.

At the end of each agenda item, I asked myself the classic reporter questions of "who, what, where, when, why, how and how much?" All I had to do was jot down a few words and when I got home to my trusty PC, I could expand those into realistic summaries of what went on. As much of the dialogue in meetings is either unnecessary, repetitive, or both, simply use your brain as a filter. That's what it's trained to do for you in your day-to-day life, so it works for meetings too. One word of warning though: don't wait too long before you work up your minutes. Another trick the brain does is to forget after a few hours or a day or so at most...

Instructions

People who buy products that require instructions, need to know how to assemble/install/use the product as easily as possible. And, because many people are technodorks like me, instructions need to be understood by the lowest common denominator.

Logically then, you might think, the best person to write instructions for technodorks like me is someone who knows every last detail about the product, how it was made, how it works, what it does, and what its inside leg measurement is. In other words, an expert.

This could not be further from the truth.

Instructions should never be written by experts.

Quite simply, experts know too much.

Consequently they are very prone to making the mistake of assuming the reader knows a little bit about the subject matter already.

To an expert, the fact that before you begin assembling the bookcase you need to align sections A, B and C with each other may be so blindingly obvious it's not even worth mentioning. To someone like me it's not just worth mentioning, it's absolutely essential if I'm not to spend the next three hours wondering why on earth I can't find any bolt holes that line up.

Equally, instructions should not be written by the sales people, the marketing executives, the guys in the lab, the production staff, or anyone else – even you – if there's a risk they might have become familiar with the subject matter. Familiarity can breed, if not contempt, at least wrongful assumptions about the audience's existing knowledge. Instruction writing must match your target audience.

Wherever practical, instructions should be written by someone who knows as much as, but no more than, the audience. For any form of instructions to be followed by non-technical users, the writer should assume zero prior knowledge and the best way to ensure s/he does that, is if s/he doesn't have any prior knowledge her/himself.

Key tips for well-written instructions:

- Approach it with logic and common sense
- Don't assume any prior knowledge on reader's part
- Start right at the beginning of the process
- Use simple, plain language in short sentences
- Use "active voice", not "passive voice" (e.g. "take the lid off now", rather than "the lid should be taken off at this point")
- Keep each step separate, no matter how simple you think it is
- If you use illustrations, make sure they're clear and uncomplicated
- If using translations, get each language version "reality checked" by a native speaker

Finally, you need to test the instructions on people who are genuinely typical of the target audience. And that means, preferably, people outside your organization. Someone in the next office may not have tried assembling the item before, but is still likely to have some prior knowledge.

Keep an open mind

Still following the same lines, for any product to be used by ordinary folks in the street, try also to get the instructions written by someone from a totally unrelated department or even from outside your organization. No matter how thoroughly you know your product, a fresh outsider's view will often pick up on ways to improve the instructions – or even to improve the product itself.

There is nothing that will blacken the name of your product and your company faster than a customer like me not being able to put your product together easily.

Although customers like me will get over it after taking a cold shower and asking the brainy next-door neighbor to interpret the instructions, we'll probably remember all those bad things next time we're shopping for the sort of products you sell. And we'll buy your competitor's.

Humor

For generations people have been saying that laughter is good medicine. And now the scientists have taken an interest, it turns out great-grandma was right. The boffins have discovered that laughter releases helpful goodies in the body which boost your immune system. In fact the therapeutic benefits of laughter are now being harnessed by academia and the business community into laughter workshops and other formalized chuckle sessions. Get the workers laughing and you raise productivity, so it seems.

However it is extremely easy to get humor wrong. And a joke that's sent to someone who doesn't see the funny side will create more ill health through raised blood pressure than a few laughs could ever cure.

So what's the answer?

How do we harness humor and make it work for us, not against us?

People often say that the internet's international nature makes it an unsuitable environment for humor for fear of it not translating across national boundaries – and inadvertently causing offense. But there are a couple of simple rules which – although not universal panaceas that always work – can help you use humor without risk.

Use humor about situations, not people. If you think about it, the butt of many jokes and other humor is a person or group of people, so it's hardly surprising that offense is caused. The more extreme types are obvious – mother-in-law jokes, blonde jokes, women jokes, men jokes – but there are many more subtle ones too.

Then there are the nationality gags. I remember in

one year hearing exactly the same joke (in three different languages) told by an American about the Polish, by a Canadian about Newfoundlanders, by a French person about Belgians, by a French-speaking Belgian about the Flemish, and by a Flemish person about the Dutch.

Laugh at circumstances, not people

Obviously most humor is going to involve people in one way or another. But as long as the butt of the joke is a situation or set of circumstances, not the people, you're far less likely to upset anyone. And there is an added advantage here. Whoever they are and wherever they come from, people will usually identify with a situation. Take this one for example...

> Some people are driving along at night and are stopped by a police car. The officer goes to the driver and warns him that one of the rear lights on his SUV isn't working. The driver jumps out and looks terribly upset. The officer reassures him that he won't get a ticket, it's just a warning, so there's no problem. "Oh yes there is a problem," says the man as he rushes towards the back of the car. "If you could see my rear lights it means I've lost my trailer."

As the butt of the joke is the broken rear light and the loss of the trailer, not the policeman or the driver, no-one can be offended. And most people can identify with how that would feel.

Avoid colloquial or figurative language

The other key issue with humor is wordplays, puns, and anything else that's based on figurative speech, slang, or jargon. The short answer is they don't work internationally. However, if the play or *double entendre* is in the concept rather than the words, it probably will work.

These may be funny to us, but would not be understood by anyone who is not a good English speaker because there is a play on the words:

- Déjà moo: The feeling that you've heard this bull before.
- The two most common elements in the universe are hydrogen and stupidity.

These, however, probably would be understood because the humor is in the concept, not in the words themselves:

- You don't stop laughing because you grow old. You grow old because you stop laughing.
- The trouble with doing something right the first time is that nobody appreciates how difficult it was.

Overall, I think it's wise to use humor as a spicy condiment in your business writing.

Just as you would with the chilli powder in cooking, use humor in moderation if you don't know the audience well... and if you know they have a very sensitive palate, don't use it at all!

Writing for translation

Everyone thought I was nuts to take on the job of writing the scripts for sales training videos for the European division of a major US car manufacturer. "You write it in English so ze boys in Detroit can understand unt approve it," giggled the German producer down the phone to me, "zen I shoot the video and do one edit. Zat's all zey vant to spend."

"Fine," I ventured. "So what's the catch?"

"Zat one edit gets voice-overs in 24 different languages," he continued, sniggering. "Ze translations are all different lengths. So your original has to work in chunks mit long gaps in English, so it can flow at 90 miles an hour in Greek. It's a bloody nightmare. Still vant to do it?"

I let out a long sigh, stared at my sparse-looking bank statement and said yes.

Here, then, is some advice based on my painfully-earned experience.

Allow for different language lengths

Strictly speaking, this is more of a design issue, but as we saw it can affect the words too.

If you intend to use the same visual template for more than one language version, ensure your design allows for differing amounts of text (or spoken speech).

Bear in mind that English is about the shortest of the world's commercial languages. So if your text is a tight fit in English, you'll be way over length in many other languages. You need up to three times as much space for some of them. So keep your English version short and sweet.

If accuracy is essential, use the lowest common denominators

Sadly, figurative speech doesn't translate. However, translators valiantly attempt to do it, often with unfortunately amusing results – especially the "automatic" translations you see offered on the internet.

My original paragraph:

> Probably the most important part of getting your writing right is to really know what makes your customers (or any other audience) tick. Customer analysis techniques are great for getting hard facts and data. But if you want to write so you touch their hearts, you need to back up the formal information with something a bit more emotional.

The Spanish translation which appeared on a South American website:

> *Probablemente la parte más importante de escribir bien es saber realmente que es lo que a sus clientes (o cualquier otra audiencia) les llama la atención. Las técnicas de análisis de clientes son buenas para poder obtener hechos e información. Pero si quiere escribir para llegar muy cerca de su corazón, usted necesita respaldar la información formal con algo emocional.*

The automatic translation back into English:

> *Probablemente the part most important to write or is to really know that is what to his clients (or any other hearing) it calls the attention to them. The techniques of analysis of clients are good to be able to obtain facts and information. But if he wants to write to arrive closely together from his heart, you need to endorse the formal information with something emocional.*

Phew. Lucky it wasn't instructions on how to carry out life-saving surgery. Had I been writing my piece for multiple languages, I would have written it like this, with simple syntax and all figurative speech stripped out:

> *To write effectively, it is most important that the writer knows the customers (or any other group the writer is writing for) very well, and understands how they think. It's possible to get useful facts and information from customer analysis techniques.*

However if the writer wants to appeal to customers emotionally, emotional writing must be added to the formal information.

Boring, isn't it? However, it wouldn't get quite so many misunderstandings, which not only can be funny, but also – in a marketing or sales context – can be costly.

Be aware of how other languages work

In the paragraph above you'll see that I've removed my beloved "you" in favor of "the writer". This is especially important if you're writing for languages like Spanish or Portuguese where often they don't talk to "you", but to the third person.

Try as far as you can to organize your grammar and syntax in the English version so that they're as simple as possible. That makes it easier for translators to get right.

Ad copy and brand names: only by the experts, please

Now, we've all heard the jokes about embarrassing advertising translations, e.g. the following, edited from a list of supposedly true stories:

- The Dairy Association's huge success with the campaign "Got Milk?" prompted them to expand advertising to Mexico. It was soon brought to their attention the Spanish translation read "Are you lactating?"
- Scandinavian vacuum manufacturer Electrolux used the following in an American campaign:

"Nothing sucks like Electrolux."

- Clairol introduced the "Mist Stick", a curling iron, into Germany only to find out that "mist" is slang for manure. Not too many people had a use for the manure stick.

- Colgate introduced a toothpaste in France called "Cue", the name of a notorious porno magazine.

- Coors put its slogan "Turn it loose" into Spanish, where it was read as "Suffer from diarrhoea."

...and so on. Whether these are true or not is debatable. But the awful thing is, they could happen for real. And if I were responsible for a hefty international marketing or ad budget, that would wipe the smile right off my face.

There are some lessons to learn here about writing for branding and marketing material in multiple languages:

1. Get the homework and background research done by appropriate experts in each and every language market you're going to. One Spanish-speaking country will have words and interpretations that are different from another. Brazilian Portuguese is different from Portuguese Portuguese. French French is slightly different from Belgian French and Swiss French and Québécois French. And that's before we even get started on languages in the Mid East, Africa, Asia and beyond.

2. Make sure your translations are done not just by translation experts in each respective language, but translation experts who understand how to write well in their own language. Insist on this when you hire the translation agency. They may think it's OK as long as they use a native-speaker of the language the text is being translated into, but normally that's not good enough.

3. It's impossible to judge the quality of translations into languages you don't speak, so get them double-checked by an appropriate native speaker. Don't leave it to the translation agency; play it safe.

Spoken words

Making a speech

The worst part of giving a speech is thinking about it beforehand

In fact, if you prepare properly, once you get started the jitters disappear. Many people say that it's good to get slightly nervous before you start because the rise in your adrenalin level puts you in peak form to perform. (But not if you're so hyped you're chewing the furniture. So prepare... and relax.)

Never use language you wouldn't use in normal conversation

That's because it makes you sound stilted, artificial, and boring. People often try to give themselves a personality transplant before they speak in public and talk as they think a public speaker "should" talk. This doesn't work, especially if you're a beginner. *Always* be yourself.

The best speakers always talk to audiences as if they were talking to a friend over a cup of coffee

This means in a natural, friendly, personal style. They make it look and sound easy, but usually that's because of the work that's gone into it beforehand. No matter how pompous or snobbish they may be in real life (think politicians) their speeches are usually natural and friendly because they know that works best.

So how do you achieve this smooth, seamless, natural style?

Start by writing yourself a list of points – a structure that includes a beginning, a middle and an end. Strengthen that structure with a few short, relevant and, above all, true stories from your own experience. Audiences appreciate honesty and, being naturally voyeuristic (in the nicest possible way) enjoy sharing your innermost experiences.

Then talk through the structure into an audio recorder

Don't worry about style or grammar at this stage, just chat it through as if you were talking to that friend over the cup of coffee. Finally rewind the tape and then transcribe it. It's a terrible job. I hate transcribing, but the benefits make all the tedium worthwhile. Talk nicely to your PA or secretary if you have one...

Now, get to work editing that transcript

Assuming it has been transcribed directly into your PC, the process should be easy. (And make a copy before you start, in case things go wrong.) Above all else, don't take out the natural pauses or less-than-grammatically-perfect-but-totally-"you"-content. Be sure, however, to clean up any sections that sound lumpy and awkward. Give the rest a gentle tidy-up.

Depending on the occasion, it helps to add in some humour to illustrate the points you make

But be careful with humor, because if it's even a little bit inappropriate for the occasion it can spoil the whole presentation. Bad or tasteless jokes take a lot of recovering from. Also, avoid humor if it isn't something you use or sympathize with normally. There's nothing worse than a joke told by someone who doesn't think it's funny.

Writing your speech, as opposed to working only from notes, stops you running under or over your allotted time slot

This can be embarrassing. By all means develop bullet points to work from, but write up in full what you're going to say before you get out there. That helps to lodge the content firmly in your mind. Well worth it.

To calculate how many words fit into a given time slot, here's the formula:

People speak at 120-150 words per minute. Multiply your speed (make a judgment on whether you speak slowly or quickly) by the number of minutes, and that's how many words you need. If you want to be particularly scientific about gauging your own speed, time a section of your taped material, mark that section on your written transcript, run a word count on it via your word processing software and then do the calculation.

Most important of all is to rehearse, rehearse, rehearse

Not too early, or you'll be fed up with the speech, but not the night before either. Never be ashamed of rehearsing. I know it's hard when your partner is waiting impatiently for you to mow the lawn, cook dinner or anything else for that matter – or your kids scream with laughter when they hear your performance from behind the bathroom door. I've been there. But tell them all to get lost, nicely, rehearse until you feel comfortable with your presentation, then go out there on the day and knock 'em dead. And enjoy!

Audio

A spoken audio track shouldn't just be confined to radio commercials. A well-written track can work wonders to liven up anything from product assembly instructions on CD, to the home page of your website or blog. The trouble is, not all spoken audio tracks are well written.

Often we think if we pay for a good voice-over artiste to record the words, by some miracle he or she will be able to transform lumpy brochure copy into a great sounding audio track. Wrong. I have directed some of the most experienced voice artistes in Europe and although I've seen them do a lot to improve a weak script, they're not magicians.

We tend to underestimate the value of the human voice in communications – a voice can convey a lot more than mere words. It can touch people's emotions in ways that text could never hope to. But you're not going to make much of an impression on people's emotions if the script for your spoken words reads like a passage from last year's Company Report and Accounts.

Remember that audio speech really is "a word in your ear"

Someone once said that audio listeners aren't one audience of thousands; they're thousands of audiences of one. Always communicate with "you" in a personal style, as if you were talking to the listener direct. Get it right, and your close proximity to the listener's ear is a powerful communication tool. Get it wrong, and you unleash the equivalent strength of hostility. Never patronize or talk down. Write as if you're talking to a friend. Be honest and realistic – no hype, no corporate-speak, no unnecessary jargon.

There's no mystique about spoken speech

It's simply that – writing the way people speak, rather than the way we've been taught to write at school. If you want see how that works, audio-record yourself talking through the topic you want to write a script about, as if to your intended audience. Transcribe it, clean it up (but not too much – audio speech must sound natural if it's going to work, unless it's a commercial) and that's about right for your script.

Use a crisp, uncluttered style

Funnily enough, people who write well for online purposes are more likely to write well for audio (and video) because those styles, like online copy, are more direct, more human. When you're writing for audio, use easy, shortish sentences, but vary their lengths. Stick to one idea per sentence where possible. Make each new idea flow logically out of the previous one.

Check everything you write by reading it aloud

No matter how relaxed a sentence may look on paper or screen, it could read awkwardly. Always, always check what you've written by reading it to yourself or preferably to someone else. Or into a recorder, so you can listen to it as often as you need. If it does read badly, change it – even if that involves doing something ungrammatical. Remember, write as people speak, even if it would make your old English teacher blanch.

Words on their own become boring

After a few minutes, wall-to-wall words begin to drone and make people's attention wander. Break it up with musical interludes. Use simple sound effects. Use pauses. For a script that's more than a few sentences long, use a second voice for contrast. Get the voices to relate to each other, bringing the audience in as the third party in a three-way conversation. Use "character voices" as well as straight-sounding narration (most good voice artistes can do numerous different accents and styles). Above all, use your imagination – audio has much more creative potential than most people realize.

Use a voice artiste to record your audio track

No matter how good you think your speaking voice is, if you haven't got the training and experience you won't come over well. Most cities have at least one voice agency in town and you can select your choice from there. Another good place to recruit is local radio stations. Their DJs and announcers, presenters and reporters usually moonlight. And it shouldn't cost much; a script of up to 15 minutes long shouldtake no more than one hour of the artiste's time.

Choose your playback medium intelligently

If you're creating an audio program to teach people how to work a machine or put some DIY decking together, make sure you offer them a playback format they can actually use. For example, even now not everyone has a portable listening device, but may have an old CD player handy to take out into the garden. If your program should be listened to in-car, remember that people with older, cheaper cars, may still have cassette players – especially in countries not quite so industrialized as the UK or the USA.

On a website, work "with" accompanying text – don't fight it or mirror it

There's no point telling people what they can already see. Use spoken words to add a dimension to the written text, or to embellish images where there is little or no text. Don't depend too heavily on the audio content to get important messages over (some people don't even have their speakers on all the time).

Above all, enjoy creating your website audio speech. If you enjoy writing it, there's a good chance your audience will enjoy listening to it. That helps a lot to achieve your objectives.

Radio Interviews

Doing a spot on local or even national radio can terrify the pants off people, but in all honesty it shouldn't. Radio is lovely; it's relaxed, low-pressure and very friendly. There's none of the hustle and bustle of television with its harsh lights and aggressive-looking equipment.

It's all very low key and informal; one time when I was interviewed about one of my books at a station in south-west England I ended up boiling the kettle and making tea for everyone while I was waiting to go on the show.

So if you're asked to be interviewed on a radio show, or to participate in a discussion or phone-in about your business or hobby, do it. Not only is it good publicity, but also it's good fun.

And although, strictly speaking, there's no writing involved here for you, it's a good idea to be aware of the basics and write down key points you want to make, so you can glance down at your notes if you need to.

My first piece of advice is, RELAX

Forget about the microphones. Forget about the headphones – you don't have to wear them unless you want to. Just talk to the interviewer as if s/he were a friend you're having a chat with over a cup of coffee.

Look him/her in the eye – these people are trained to encourage interviewees visually with nods and smiles, so it will be easy to connect with him/her. When you do, that will come over in your voice and what you say.

A small technical point

Try, if you can, to avoid talking over the presenter/ interviewer and anyone else on the show. In normal conversation we often do this, usually just by saying a word or two in agreement (or disagreement) with another person. However, on radio more than one voice speaking at a time comes across as very messy and hard to hear. If you're asked a question, wait until the speaker stops before you say anything and, when you've finished, end your statement very clearly by shutting up!

Promoting a business – or not?

Another piece of advice is, if you're being interviewed in connection with anything to do with your business, forget giving them a description of what you *do*. What a radio audience (and any prospective clients out there) are interested in – the only thing they're interested in – is what you could *do for them*.

Let's say you're a Virtual Assistant and you're given the opportunity to describe your work briefly on the show.

Think: what are the main benefits a client gets from using your VA service? When you work for someone, what differences does that make to their lives? More quality time with their kids? More time to concentrate on their own skillset? More time to get out and sell, so increasing profits? Do you free people up so they can do more of what they're really good at? Do you handle the quantity, so they can get going with more quality?

In, say, a 45-second slot, aim for a statement of about 70 words. Don't try to be slick or overly clever; just be sincere. Write out what you want to say, memorize it, then put the piece of paper away. When you do your interview, remember the gist of that message and say it naturally in your own words.

And above all else, enjoy it!

Video

As technology moves us further and further on in what we can achieve with relatively simple kit, we can be grateful that decent quality video has finally become affordable for nearly everyone.

With video cameras being so easy to use and video material being so easy to upload, it's not surprising that many people think it's equally easy to produce good video content and performance. However, they're wrong.

Whereas there are high-tech, high-quality solutions for all the practical elements of making a video, once it comes to who says what and how, no amount of technology can improve on a bad performance.

The camera exaggerates even the slightest movement and makes it look maniacal. On the other hand, once you recognize this point and make yourself sit absolutely bolt still, you'll look like a ventriloquist's dummy. It takes a lot of training and practice to hit the right balance, as any TV newsreader will tell you.

The answer?

Unless you happen to be very good at on-camera presenting, don't do it. Instead use the off-camera interview technique.

This technique is often used on TV by news reporters and documentary directors, where you see the interviewee talking to an unseen someone just beside the camera. It's brilliant for two reasons: one, the camera in this case is recording one half of a genuine conversation between two people which is far more natural and relaxed than a "talking head"; and two, you don't have to remember your lines in anything like the same detail.

All it needs is for someone to sit beside the camera (or it can be the person running the camera, depending on whether you use remote control or not) and ask you questions which you will have pre-agreed, but not over-rehearsed.

You then look at the person (so your eyeline ends just to one side of the camera) and reply to him or her. The person's questions can then be cut out afterwards, or if you really like the "fly-on-the-wall" approach, you can leave them in.

Whoever asks the questions must take care not to phrase them in such a way that you automatically respond with either a "yes" or a "no" as this can make the dialogue fall rather flat. The way to avoid that is to ask "open" questions and these are what journalists use. Start every question with:

What...?
Who...?
Where...?
Why...?
When...?
Which...?
How...?

And finally, leave a short gap between the question and your answer so that if you decide to edit out the questions later, it can be done cleanly. Similarly, don't talk over each other as that can mess up the soundtrack.

Be careful with sound quality

Another damning element of DIY videos can be that the voice of the speaker sounds like s/he was talking from the bottom of a well – echoing, hollow and distorted. This usually arises when you are using the camera microphone to record the sound; no matter how much camera manufacturers swear up and down that their on-camera mics are of excellent quality, in the main they are not.

Rather than go to the expense and palaver of setting up individual mics, you can simply ensure that the place where you record your video is as sound-dead as possible. A nice, fluffy, thickly carpeted, softly furnished living room is ideal, well away from domestic noises. Avoid shooting in large open spaces, outdoors, and anywhere with hard floors and few soft furnishings.

Minitipz

- Before you start to write, be sure you've done your homework including:
  - Define what your message must achieve
  - Get to know your audience very well
  - Understand how people will receive your message
  - Develop your message out of the right criteria (what do they need to hear, not just what you want to tell them)
- Write as people speak, but don't just write down a conversation
- Write in terms of "we" and "us" or "I" and "me," but don't use a pompous "royal we" approach
- Make every sentence relevant to the audience – "what's in it for them?"
- Wherever possible write to "you" – not to third-person "customers", "staff", "suppliers", etc.
- Don't just get to the point – start with it, and phrase it so it will grab the audience's attention
- Say what you mean and don't procrastinate with fuzzy language
- Be informal, but be careful not to be overly familiar
- Use go words, not slow words – sharper nouns, stronger, shorter verbs
- Use active rather than passive phrasing ("go to bed now", not "it's time you went to bed")

- Although simple is usually better, don't over-simplify – it can seem childish or patronising
- Don't go into more than one idea per sentence
- Write so that one sentence flows logically into the next
- One-word or verbless sentences are useful for pacing and effect, but only if you use them sparingly
- Where possible, start new paragraphs with links like "Of course," or "However," to keep the audience hooked
- Use a list or bullet points to put across more than two or three items in a sequence
- Keep jargon to a minimum and be sure your audience will understand what you do use
- Avoid meaningless or valueless clichés because they make your writing seem unoriginal
- Learn the difference between poor clichés and your business's commonly used terms, and use the latter intelligently
- Avoid adjectives and superlatives that smell phoney, e.g. "best", "fastest", "exciting"
- Use the most visual adjectives and adverbs you can think of – they're powerful
- Use "Plain English" wherever possible and especially when writing for audiences whose mother-tongue is not English

- Especially with online text but with print too, avoid long blocks of text because they're uninviting to read
- Visually break up continuous sections of text by peppering them with cross-headings or emboldened key points
- Keep online sentences and paragraphs short, and vary the length of offline sentences
- Check for small grammatical and punctuation goofs – they make you look amateurish
- Check for spelling mistakes and don't rely totally on your spellchecker
- Proofread your work backwards – it sounds crazy but you don't miss spelling mistakes that way

Spoken speech

- To get a true idea of your own natural speech style, tape record yourself talking to someone in an appropriate context and then transcribe it
- Write in the style of the transcribed text (or a style that feels comfortable for you to say) – not how some people think "public speaking" should be phrased
- Even if you want to make a formal impression on the audience, avoid long words – especially unfamiliar ones you could trip over when your stage nerves are making you edgy

- Always write shorter sentences than you do for text, vary the length of them, and never follow one longish sentence with another

- When in doubt, read it aloud – if there's anything awkward you'll feel yourself tripping over it

- Don't use long, or even short, qualifying clauses – they work on paper or screen but not in spoken speech. Try reading this aloud: "The way forward, although not necessarily what was intended by our parent company, is to buy more components from Thailand." Sounds odd, doesn't it? Turn it around instead: "This is not necessarily what was intended by our parent company, but the way forward is to buy more components from Thailand."

- If you list a number of items, reprise your initial thought about them afterwards or there'll be an awkward jump. Try reading this aloud: "It's taken three months of co-ordinated effort by HR, marketing, sales, distribution, logistics, warehousing, finance and customer service to achieve our objectives." Falls off a cliff, doesn't it? Now add a reprise: "It's taken three months of co-ordinated effort by HR, marketing, sales, distribution, logistics, warehousing, finance and customer service – all these, working together to achieve our objectives."

I hope you've enjoyed this book and find it helpful in your business writing.

As ever, please feel free to get in touch with me if you have any comments or questions and I'll do my best to respond appropriately.

With all good wishes,

Suze

HowToWriteBetter.net

suze@suzanstmaur.com

MINITIPZ

HowToWriteBetter

*Suze's fast-growing online resource for all you
need to know about business and social writing*

Suze started the website "HowToWriteBetter" early in
2011, since when it has grown into a popular meeting
place for everyone who wants to boost their writing
success for business, social and creative pursuits –
including English-as-a-second-language speakers who
come to the site to find out what really works in
written English communications.

Here you'll find more than 200 free articles on how to
write better, including guest posts from well-known
experts on various specialized forms of writing – plus a
useful range of Suze's books for you to choose from.
It's a site well worth bookmarking.

Visit HowToWriteBetter soon if you haven't already;
you'll be very welcome and pleased to find such a mine
of helpful information at your fingertips.

Go to *http://www.howtowritebetter.net*

Books by Suzan St Maur

The A to Z of Video and AV Jargon, Routledge

Writing Words That Sell (with John Butman), Management Books 2000

Writing Your Own Scripts and Speeches, McGraw Hill

How To Write Winning Non-fiction, Publishing Academy

How To Sell Yourself In Writing, HowToWriteBetter.net

Business Writing Made Easy, Bookshaker

Get Yourself Published, Lean Marketing Press

Powerwriting, Prentice Hall Business

English To English: the A to Z of British/American translations, Bookshaker

Banana Skin Words and how not to slip on them, HowToWriteBetter.net

How To Laugh Your Way Through Cancer: 101 cancer-related tips guaranteed to help you grin (and bear it) Bookshaker

The Horse Lover's Joke Book, Kenilworth Press

The Pony Lover's Joke Book, Kenilworth Press

Canine Capers, Kenilworth Press

The Food Lover's Joke Book, ItsCooking.com

The Country Lover's Joke Book, Merlin Unwin Books

The Jewellery Book (with Norbert Streep), Magnum

The Home Safety Book, Jill Norman Books

Wedding Speeches For Women, How To Books

The A to Z of Wedding Wisdom, How To Books

How To Get Married In Green, How To Books

Planning A Winter Wedding, How To Books

SUZAN ST MAUR

Canadian born Suzan "Suze" St Maur has worked as an advertising copywriter, script and speech writer since the 1970s, as well as researching and writing nearly 30 published non-fiction books – with several more in the pipeline.

Her key area of expertise is writing for business and general non-fiction, where she helps people produce more effective written material of their own, more quickly – from entire books down to micro-blogging.

Via Suze's website and blog, *HowToWrite Better.net*, you'll find a large selection of books, eBooks, articles and blog posts on how to improve your writing skills for business and pleasure, including:

- *Powerwriting: the hidden skills you need to transform your business writing* (print book)
- *How To Write Winning Non-fiction: the complete writing and publishing handbook for non-fiction authors* (print book and Kindle)
- *How To Sell Yourself In Writing* (eBook)
- *Banana Skin Words and how not to slip on them* (eBook)
- *Super Speeches: how to write and deliver them well* (eBook)
- *English to English: the ultimate glossary of British vs USA words* (eBook)

* 9 7 8 1 9 0 7 4 9 8 8 3 1 *